Activity-Based Management in Government

by

Joseph Kehoe
William Dodson
Robert Reeve
Gustav Plato

Coopers & Lybrand L.L.P.
Washington, DC

Joseph Kehoe, William Dodson, Robert Reeve, Gustav Plato

Activity-Based Management in Government

Library of Congress Catalog No. 94-068988

ISBN 0-944533-10-8

Bulk quantities of this book may be obtained from:

Bookmasters, Inc.
Distribution Center
1444 State Rt. 42
RD 11
Mansfield, Ohio 44903
Telephone: 1-800-247-6553
Fax: 419-281-6883

40362

OTHER BOOKS AND MONOGRAPHS PUBLISHED OR DISTRIBUTED BY COOPERS & LYBRAND'S PUBLISHING DIVISION

Managing Change: Opening Organizational Horizons, 1994

Innovation: The Creativity Jogger, 1994

Customer Service Measurement, 1994

Survey Assessment, 1994

Excellence in Government: Total Quality Management in the 1990s. Second Edition, 1992

Process Improvement: A Guide For Teams, 1993

BreakPoint Business Process Redesign, 1992

(For more information on these titles, see Appendix A)

Table of Contents

Acknowledgments

We deeply appreciate the help of organizations and individuals who, directly through interviews or indirectly by our working with them, lent a hand in preparing this book on Activity-Based Management. They include the following:

Organizations

U.S. Air Force
        Space and Missile Systems Center, Material Command
City of Indianapolis, IN, Department of Capital Asset Management
Consortium for Advanced Manufacturing International (CAM-I)
U.S. Defense Mapping Agency, Washington, DC
EG&G Mound Applied Technologies, Inc., Miamisburg, OH
The George Washington University, Washington, DC
Hughes Aircraft, Corporate Finance Office, Los Angeles, CA
U.S. Internal Revenue Service
        Baltimore, MD District Office
        Managing Accounts Core Business System Office,
        Washington, DC
        Office of Cost Management, Washington, DC
        Value Tracking Core Business System Office,
        Washington, DC
National Performance Review, Executive Office of the Vice President of the United States

U.S. Navy
>Naval Sea Systems Command, Shipyard Directorate
>(NAVSEA 07), Washington, DC
>Charleston Naval Shipyard, Charleston, SC
>Mare Island Naval Shipyard, Vallejo, CA
>Norfolk Naval Shipyard, Norfolk, VA
>Pearl Harbor Naval Shipyard, Pearl Harbor, HI
>Portsmouth Naval Shipyard, Kittery, ME
>Puget Sound Naval Shipyard, Bremerton, WA

City of Phoenix, AZ, City Auditor's Office
U.S. Postal Service
>Finance Department, Washington, DC
>Office of the Treasurer, Washington, DC

Individuals

A special word of thanks to these pioneers in using Activity-Based Management in government and among government contractors, who readily shared with us their insights and materials:

David Armstrong, Peggy Bianco, Thomas Carroll, A. Anthony Ciotola, Robert Chapman, James Flanagan, Dale Geiger, Robert L. Griffiths, John Kamensky, Stephen Kearney, Morgan Kinghorn, RADM Thomas Porter, Sri Kant Sastry, Susan Savard, Michael Serlin, Wayne Simpson, Angelo Wider, Clif Williams, and Peter Zampino.

Coopers & Lybrand

We appreciate the fine technical insights of our Coopers & Lybrand advisers: Partners Jim Dillard, Mike Mayer, Charles Porter, and Bill Trahant, and professional staff Charles Brown, Dennis Burke, Cliff Cooksey, Robert Eckman, Kathleen Leibfried, Joe McMahon, Andy Olson, Mo Treadway, Judy Wade, and Susan Williams.

Finally, this book would not have been possible without the superb work of publisher Don Stoufer, project manager and writer/editor Steve Clyburn, writers Joy Mara and Mary Anne Reilly, production manager Mike Clover, word processing coordinator Ana Fano, senior word processor/editor Lucia Gladchtein, graphic designers Kim Farcot and Patrick Scroggins, and the editorial services of Grammarians, Inc.

Introduction

This is a book for government executives and managers. We wrote it to help you answer tough management questions:

- **Reorganizing:** "Which parts of my organization should be consolidated or decentralized? What work should be done in-house, and what should be outsourced?"

- **Right-sizing:** "How do you size an organization for future work load?"

- **Energizing:** "How do we reenergize stalled improvement initiatives like Total Quality, and set them on the right track?"

- **Measuring performance:** "How do we measure progress in improvement programs and the value of the results they produce?"

- **Managing costs:** "How do we define, identify, and eliminate work that adds no value to our products and services? How do we know our value added work is cost-effective?"

- **Improving controls:** "How do we improve operational and financial controls to reduce risks for the organization and its customers?"

- **Competing:** "How do we compete against other public and private organizations that want to take over our mission and services? How do we develop accurate cost data for competitive bids?"

- **Pricing:** "How do we ensure full cost recovery for goods and services we sell to the public or other agencies?"

Hundreds of private companies use activity-based costing (ABC) and Activity-Based Management to answer these questions. As with other books on these subjects, we could simply tell you what those companies did. But, as you know, there are both subtle and glaring differences between the management challenges of industry and those of government.

Instead, we will show you how national and local public sector organizations have applied activity costing and activity management to the task of reinventing government. Our examples range from one of the nation's largest employers, the U.S. Postal Service, to a road maintenance department in Indianapolis. They include defense organizations like the Navy's shipyards, and civilian agencies such as the U.S. Internal Revenue Service.

We want you to come away from our book understanding what these organizations discovered—that four things were missing from their earlier attempts to improve performance. They were as follows:

- Financial and performance information systems that enable and encourage managers to make strategic process improvements that maximize value to customers and taxpayers.

- A management and organizational structure built around processes, or how work gets done in an organization.

- A strategy for managing the human aspects of changing from a static bureaucracy to a dynamic, improvement-driven organization.

- A common financial and managerial language for different parts of an organization and all of a government's agencies.

Ours is not a "how-to" book for adding these missing elements to your management improvement initiatives. How you apply the approaches we outline depends on your organization's needs, culture, environment, and the nature of your work. Also, ABC is still evolving: nearly every organization that applies it discovers new uses. These go far beyond ABC's original purpose of calculating accurate product costs, all the way to Activity-Based Management, a comprehensive management approach we discuss in this book.

But don't think that progress has stopped there. As more public organizations adopt activity costing and management, expect to see them improving the methods we discuss and inventing new ones. Many pioneers are traveling on this road and we invite you to join them.

Joseph Kehoe
William Dodson
Robert Reeve
Gustav Plato

Coopers & Lybrand L.L.P.

How To Use This Book

Because this book is written for government managers and executives, we focused on what they need and want to know about activity costing and management. This starts with the value activity-based costing (ABC) adds to management decision-making, and ends with how to introduce and sustain ABC and Activity-Based Management.

Our book includes more information on introducing ABC to an organization than do most other books on the subject, and emphasizes public sector organizations. It has somewhat less information on the accounting calculations of ABC, which are well covered by the reference books listed in Appendix A. We offer a word of caution about these other books, however. Most report on the ABC cost accounting and financial management systems developed for manufacturing companies, with few examples from service or government operations. Still, some address services, and all are good technical references.

Readers who want an *overview* of activity costing and management can get this by reading Chapter 1 and skimming Chapters 2 and 3. *Technical details* on ABC may be found in Part II. If your organization is contemplating *restructuring* or faces *major budget cuts*, read Chapter 8 closely. If your organization charges a *fee for service* or works under a *revolving fund or enterprise fund*, then Chapter 5, on cost assignment, will be very important. If you are going *to introduce activity costing or management*, then it is critical that you read the entire book and pay close attention to Part IV.

The following will give you an overview of each chapter. Also, our index is designed to give you quick access to information on any specific government organization or technical topic.

Part I: Introduction to Activity Costing and Management

This first part introduces government executives and managers to the uses and benefits of ABC and Activity-Based Management.

Chapter 1 provides an overview of activity costing and management concepts and how they are applied in government. In this chapter, we contrast these with traditional cost accounting and management approaches.

Chapter 2 offers a brief history of activity costing and management. Its purpose is to show that ABC has successfully changed managers' thinking from a narrow, functional view to a modern process perspective of operations.

Chapter 3 shows how ABC complements Total Quality Management, time-based management, reengineering, and benchmarking. Even if you decide not to introduce Activity-Based Management, we hope this chapter shows that ABC can, by itself, improve results of other management approaches and methods.

Part II: Building Blocks of Activity-Based Costing

Chapters 4, 5, and 6 outline the technical aspects of ABC as it is applied in government operations, while Chapter 7 shows how to run an individual ABC project or introduce ABC to control and information systems. These chapters provide sufficient information for a reader who is new to ABC to understand its principles and methods. Those who want more technical details should use the reference books listed in Appendix A.

Chapter 4 shows how to construct an activity dictionary for an organization and explains the importance of process thinking.

Chapter 5 discusses methods of assigning costs to activities, understanding what causes these costs, and developing accurate cost estimates for products and services.

Chapter 6 lists and describes several types of studies done that, with ABC, produce information to control and improve operations.

Chapter 7 shows how to introduce and manage an ABC project and how ABC can be used to enhance control systems. This chapter closes with a discussion of how to integrate ABC into financial and management information systems.

Part III: Activity-Based Management

This section shows how organizations use Activity-Based Management to reorganize their operations, then manage them under a new set of principles.

Chapter 8 is an overview of the principles of Activity-Based Management and includes information on this approach to process-based management and performance measurement methods.

Chapter 9 provides examples of how government organizations have restructured using activity cost and management information for guidance and how they operate under this new management approach.

Chapter 10 shows how government contractors use and benefit from ABC and provides an example of one company's restructuring program. It also discusses special issues in government contractor accounting.

Part IV: Initiating Activity Costing and Management

Our concluding section explores how successful organizations manage the change from traditional management to ABC and Activity-Based Management. It includes a planning and implementation framework that covers both the technical and human aspects of change management.

Chapter 11 provides an overview of the human aspects of change management as it applies to introducing activity costing and management.

Chapter 12 is a comprehensive implementation approach that addresses all aspects of introducing and sustaining Activity-Based Management.

Appendices

Appendix A lists books on subjects such as ABC, quality management, and change management that complement and supplement this volume.

Appendix B is a list of questions that are useful to ask when planning how to introduce ABC or Activity-Based Management.

Writing Your Own Management Rules

At each chapter's end you will find a page to write down old rules and practices of public management, and new, personal principles about managing by activity. Doing this will help you customize a chapter's information to your organization.

List of Acronyms

ABC: Activity-based costing (see Glossary)
AFDC: Aid For Families of Dependent Children
BPR: Business process redesign or reengineering (see Glossary)
CAM-I: Consortium of Advanced Manufacturing International
CBS: Core business systems
CEO: Chief Executive Officer
CFO: Chief Financial Officer
COQ: Cost of quality (see Glossary)
CSF: Critical success factors (see Glossary)
DMWL: Do more with less
DOE: U.S. Department of Energy
FTE: Full-time equivalents (see Glossary)
GE: General Electric
HVAC: Heating, ventilation, and air conditioning
IRS: U.S. Internal Revenue Service
IS: Information system
JIT: Just-In-Time
NAVFAC: Naval Facilities Engineering Command
NAVSEA: Naval Sea Systems Command
TBM: Time-based management
3M: Minnesota Mining and Manufacturing Co.
TQM: Total Quality Management
WBS: Work breakdown structure

PART I

INTRODUCTION TO ACTIVITY COSTING AND MANAGEMENT

Chapter

1

Meeting New Challenges With New Principles

- Public managers work in mazes of rules, practices, and procedures that prevent them from doing what is best for their country, state, or community. Simply eliminating some of the rules is not enough to meet the challenges of an era of fiscal desperation and taxpayer anger.

- New approaches—activity costing and management—create a new set of principles for creating and managing cost-effective, high-quality government service.

- These approaches are a way to tear down the mazes so that government managers can finally take charge of improving their operations.

- New government accounting standards will almost certainly include activity costing.

"We can no longer afford to pay more—and get less from—our government."
—Bill Clinton and Al Gore,
Putting People First

This is a book about cost-effective, high-performance government service. In it you will see how public organizations and their contractors use activity-based costing (ABC) and Activity-Based Management to control and improve operations. ABC gives managers the information they need for sound business decisions, while Activity-Based Management provides an organizational framework for acting on those decisions.

The Old Rules of Public Management

It used to be that the rules of public management were simple:

> *Accomplish missions as well as or just a bit better than the year before, avoid scandal, stay within budget, and follow procedures.*

Public managers who did these things looked forward to good careers. Unless caught in a sudden shift in the political winds, their agency was either ramping up, staying steady, or in slow decline. Budget and staff cuts happened, but they were mainly annoying, not devastating. Minor ones could be handled with a little belt-tightening and staff attrition. Major ones might mean moving to another agency that was on the upswing. Life as a career public servant was predictable and secure.

Although most public managers thought their budgets should be larger, few focused on cost effectiveness, the return that taxpayers were receiving on their investment in government. One reason was that most managers were not held accountable for being cost-effective in their decisions. Instead, governments created vast volumes of rules and regulations that were intended to promote effective spending, but that often prevented management action for improvement. Further, even if the average public manager wanted to do a better job at controlling costs, he or she did not have the appropriate financial or operations performance information for sound, business-like decisions.

Things have changed. Burgeoning entitlement payments and Cold War defense spending created huge federal deficits. Taxpayer revolts and dwindling federal support are cutting state and local programs to (and sometimes through) the bone. From Washington to your own home town, lawmakers are reducing all discretionary funding and total operations budgets across the board. The pressure this puts on agency and department budgets is enormous and unprecedented in U.S. public service history.

At the same time, complaints about government effectiveness have risen from a murmur to a roar. According to Vice President Al Gore, analysis of public opinion poll data shows that in 1965, more than 60 percent of citizens thought that government generally tries to do the right thing. By 1994, only 10 percent agreed that the statement is true.[1]

Recently, many elected officials lost their jobs because of such citizen distrust. The lesson has not been lost on the survivors and their new, reform-minded colleagues. All are deeply concerned with government management and are taking steps to create fundamental changes in public administration.

The New Rules

In this last decade of the 20th century, almost every initiative to reform government emphasizes cost effectiveness. Take, for example, just two of many recent federal laws concerning government operations. At the core of both the Chief Financial Officers Act of 1992 and the Government Performance and Results Act of 1993 are requirements for better cost management, including providing managers with better cost information. As you will see in this book, both will require ABC and Activity-Based Management to be successful.

Activity: A unit of work that has identifiable starting and ending points, that consumes resources (inputs) and produces outputs. In ABC, an activity is synonymous with a simple process, as the latter term is used in quality management and reengineering.

Activity-based costing (ABC): A set of management information and accounting methods used to identify, describe, assign costs to, and otherwise report on the operations in an organization.

Activity-based management: Business management in which process owners have the responsibility and authority to control and improve operations, and that uses ABC methods.

A few chief executives, from the White House to city hall, have also set in motion fundamental changes in their governments' approach to cost management. Aimed at reinventing the federal government, the National Performance Review's many reports read like textbooks on cost control, customer service, and competition. One of the Review's initiatives, a reformation of federal cost accounting standards, has circulated for comment a recommendation that agencies strongly consider adopting ABC:

> The Federal Accounting Standards Advisory Board notes in particular that activity-based costing has gained broad acceptance by manufacturing and service industries as an effective managerial tool. The Board encourages government entities to study its potential within their own operations.[2]

Other Board draft recommendations, including those on full costing and intergovernment transfers, will require approaches like ABC to be successful and useful. What is most important is the Board's stated intent to make cost accounting a tool for management decisions about quality and cost effectiveness.

We will invent a government that puts people first, by:
- Cutting unnecessary spending
- Serving its customers
- Empowering its employees
- Helping communities solve their own problems
- Fostering excellence

Here's how. We will:
- Create a clear sense of mission
- Steer more, row less
- Delegate authority and responsibility
- Replace regulations with incentives
- Develop budgets based on outcomes
- Expose federal operations to competition
- Search for market, not administrative, solutions
- Measure our success by customer satisfaction

Principles of the National Performance Review

Activity-Based Management is one of the core components of the City of Indianapolis' competition program, in which City departments compete with private contractors to provide local public services. The program is tough and has led City agencies to find ways to drastically cut costs while improving services. Where once only finance and accounting personnel understood the rules of cost management, now even road repair crews learn to use them when developing competitive bids. They must, to keep their jobs.

"Survival of the fittest" may overstate the intent of the new rules of cost-effective government. Instead, the intent is the survival of those who can change from following the old rules to producing results under the new ones. Let's explore some of these new rules now.

Figure 1-1
Suggested New
Principles of
Managing Public
Operations

- Find and eliminate or reduce resources devoted to non-value added activity.

- Know what activities, products, and services really cost, and understand what drives that cost.

- Know how your activities relate to each other, and how they create and fulfill demands.

- Before introducing new technology, understand how your activities work now and how you want them to work in the future.

- When improving processes and activities, think and act across functional and departmental boundaries.

- Major process improvement depends on managers having accurate financial information on their processes.

To start changing, you need a new set of management principles. We suggest a few in this first chapter to get you started and to introduce activity costing and management, but to produce results, you will have to write down and live by your own principles. You'll find space to do this at the end of each chapter.

About "do more with less"

"Do more with less," or DMWL, is one of the primary management principles in our age of shrinking budgets. The term DMWL by itself, however, can be vague and misleading. Follow it, and often you end up doing the same wrong things as before, only faster and cheaper, and reducing resources to do the right things. Let's look for a better principle. U.S. Navy shipyards faced the DMWL challenge in spades after the end of the Cold War, when Congress dictated huge budget and staff cuts. Shipyard executives knew that the "fat" in their operations wasn't due to people sitting around idle. Everyone was busy doing something. The problem was that there was no objective way to determine if everything being done was really necessary.

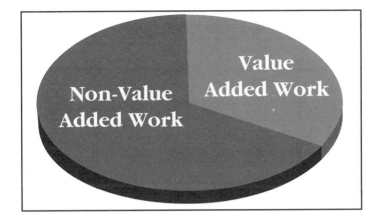

Figure 1-2
Non-value added work can consume two-thirds of an organization's resources.

Value analysis: An analysis that categorizes activities according to whether they add value to the output of an activity or process. Value added activities transform work-in-process in ways that customers perceive as beneficial. Non-value added activities either do not transform work-in-process, or transform it in ways that customers do not perceive as beneficial.

Here's the activity management solution the shipyards used: stop doing non-value added work. A business activity, or the way work is done, adds value when, in the eyes of customers, it increases the worth of products and services. Non-value activities include finding and correcting mistakes, producing reports no one reads, and following rules that don't make sense. Eliminating or reducing resources devoted to them frees money for services that increase customer satisfaction.

So, one new management principle is: "Find and eliminate or reduce resources devoted to non-value added activity." To do this, you need to use the method called value analysis, described in Chapter 6 of this book.

About competition

Lawmakers and top government executives are promoting two types of competition with great enthusiasm: public/private and public/public.

Public/private competition is nothing new to most public managers. Today its resurgence has teeth, however, and a few new twists. Indianapolis, Indiana, is a good example. In 1992, Stephen Goldsmith was elected mayor with a strong promise to reform local government through marketplace competition. He directed the City Department of Transportation to set up competitions between City road repair crews and private contractors. He also made it plain that "gaming" the numbers would not be allowed; auditors would check the City bids before they were submitted.

DOT managers knew their direct costs, but actual "full cost" figures were distorted. This was due to the traditional accounting practice of evenly allocating indirect or overhead expenses, usually by putting a multiplier on direct labor hours. This allocation approach to overhead overstated DOT's costs and made it difficult to discover what caused them.

DOT found the answer in ABC. Among other things, ABC traces the relevant costs, both direct and indirect, of operating an activity or producing a unit of output. It also helps you understand what factors or events drive those costs, so you can identify their root causes.

Says Mayor Goldsmith, "Activity-based costing has to come in front of competition because we can't even get our own folks into a bid mentality until we know how much it costs to provide a service."[3] Once they got into that mental set, though, City employees became hard-nosed businesspersons, and they have won most of their competitions. Indianapolis won, too, because the cost of road repairs dropped by as much as 60 percent.

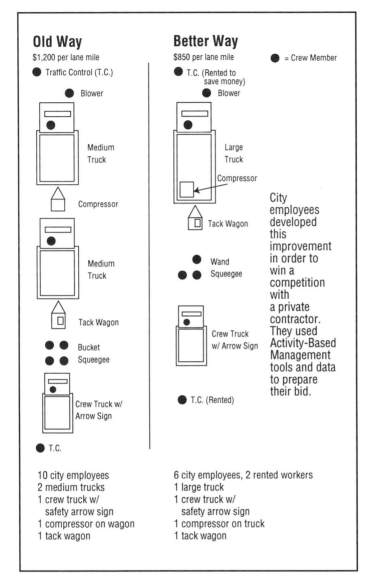

Figure 1-3
Improvements in
Crack Sealing
Process
City of
Indianapolis, 1994

That's the new public/private competition. Public/public competition now comes in two forms. The old familiar one is when another agency tries to gobble up your mission or your customers. A lot of that goes on in government right now because many agencies are "hungry" and customers are open to cost-effective proposals. This is especially true for organizations operating under revolving or enterprise funds because the era of internal monopolies is drawing to a close.

The emerging form of public/public competition is a method of shared services called franchising, in which line managers can purchase support services from their own or other agencies. These include the full range of support functions, as can be seen in Figure 1-4. A stated goal of franchising is "to create competition in the provision of these services as a way of reducing duplication and providing economies."[4]

Figure 1-4
List of Potential
Federal
Franchise
Service Areas

- Alternate dispute resolution
- Personnel
- Budget preparation
- Printing and reproduction
- Employee health care
- Procurement
- Engineering
- Quality assurance
- Facility management
- Security
- Finance and accounting
- Training
- Information technology
- Travel
- Logistics
- Worker's Compensation
- Payroll

Source: *Franchising: Essential Information*, National Performance Review.

If you manage a support service, franchising is good news when you can deliver top value and bad when you can't. Activity costing and management will help you discover how to reduce costs and to calculate the "fee" you will charge for your services. If you're a line manager looking for support services, activity costing and management will help you understand in-house cost and value before you comparison shop outside.

A new public management principle we can derive from competition is: *"Know what activities, products, and services really cost, and understand what drives that cost."* It's a simple rule but one that most organizations can't follow because nearly all forms of cost accounting used in the public and private sectors don't give you the necessary information. ABC can, as you will see in Chapters 4 and 5.

About restructuring

Opening or closing facilities, consolidating or decentralizing operations, outsourcing, downsizing, or simply moving things around to meet new priorities — these are routine events in government today. Routine, yes, but only a few organizations are doing these things with full knowledge of what is going where and with what impact. They do not have the tools to answer these tough questions:

- *"What, exactly, should we move?"* This applies especially to closing bases and facilities because most have a few programs or because program elements that must be moved elsewhere. Most organizations have to answer this question with vague and misleading information from budget line items or head counts. For example, a particular operation may require 10 people. When told to move the operation from his or her department to another, a department manager is likely to say, "It takes only six people, and that's how many I'm giving up." The department manager on the receiving end of this transfer soon discovers to his or her chagrin that this is not enough people to carry out the new operation effectively.

- *"What, exactly, are we now?"* This question often comes up after several departments or entire agencies have been consolidated. Top managers of the new organization ask this question because they have no idea of the new missions they have acquired, the duplications in support functions, or what products and services are produced or customers served. The better question, asked well in advance of a consolidation, would be "What do we want to become?"

- *"If we consolidate (or decentralize) support services, how much of each type do we need in the field and at central locations?"* Information technology and the potential for economies of scale make this type of restructuring very appealing. Unfortunately, many organizations do it without understanding how support service resources are consumed at both headquarters and field offices. Even those that do consider this all too often don't look for ways to streamline support services before restructuring them.

- *"How do we align resource needs with changing work loads?"* For defense agencies, this usually means less work. For civilian organizations, work load can rapidly go up or down, especially in competitions such as those described earlier. Either way, many agencies do not realize that changes in work loads have different effects on different functions and departments. For example, reduction in demand for a service, such as maintaining military equipment, will probably mean fewer line employees in workshops. But how many fewer people will be needed in audit, human resources, and contracting functions? Most agencies can answer that only with guesses.

ABC overcomes these problems by providing hard, objective information about operations and their costs. It starts by developing an activity model that shows the major business functions and processes of an organization, unit, or operation, and all the activities that fall under or support them. With the model, you see the relationship of activities and spot overlaps, redundancies, and missing elements. This helps to show you what and how much has to move, stay, or change.

Next, you calculate the volume of demand for a specific activity's outputs (the products and services it produces) by other activities or customers. If demand goes up or down by a certain percentage, you have a starting point for determining the new level of resources—labor, material, supplies, and so on—the activity will require. What is important is that you have precise information on a specific activity, which means that you can increase or decrease resources for only that activity. You do not, as most agencies do now, have to resort to across-the-board budget cuts for all activities in all departments.

From this, we derive another new management principle: *"Know how your activities relate to each other, and how they create and fulfill demands."* This is quite different from knowing your budget and head count. It is, in fact, the underlying theme of this book. Chapter 9 focuses on the technical aspects of restructuring, with examples from the U.S. Internal Revenue Service (IRS) and the Navy's shipyards, while Chapter 10 discusses how government contractors use activity costing and management to realign their operations with new demands.

About new technology and reengineering

The owner of the Macy's department stores used to say, "I know we're wasting half our advertising money, but we don't know which half." This is very close to the truth about how technology is applied in both the public and private sectors. A major reason is "brute force" automation, which means automating every part of a work process without considering cost effectiveness or whether some parts are non-value added. At the opposite extreme is the misguided reengineering slogan, "Obliterate, don't automate." It leads some organizations to rip out old processes without considering how they relate to others, causing major gaps and missing elements in services.

Many attempts to apply technology in public organizations are made without full understanding of the way things work. This is especially true when organizations are automating support services, which rarely have adequate documentation of their activities. Mapping existing operations is often done by systems engineers, who are prone to skimp on this task. (They would rather closet themselves to work on the "perfect" new system.)

In an ABC approach to automation, the managers and employees who work in a process first map all its activities. Such "as-is" maps allow you to see the relationships among activities and to eliminate non-value added activities. Accurate activity cost information also helps determine the cost effectiveness of automating a task versus leaving it as a manual procedure. These maps and information prevent brute force automation and "losing" a vital activity during reengineering. Developing "to-be" activity maps based on how new technology will alter work processes alerts you to changes in resource consumption, personnel requirements, and lines of authority.

As-is process model: A verbal or graphic description of a process as it is now being done, sometimes accompanied by information on the process' cost, cycle time, or other measures of performance. A to-be process model describes how the process will look and perform once it is changed.

From this we can posit another new management principle: *"Before introducing new technology, understand how your activities work now and how you want them to work in the future."* If you think public agencies always follow this rule, consider the hundreds of millions of dollars government has wasted on technology investment.

About process improvement

Most federal departments and many state and local governments have attempted some form of quality management or reengineering. Some of these initiatives have been more successful than others, but in general all have been slow to produce significant results. Typical quality projects in public agencies focus on some minor improvement within a single function or department. Even when the projects succeed, they fail to impress executives and customers because they deliver neither large savings nor major improvement.

> **Process:** A set of logically related activities done to achieve a defined business outcome, such as to produce a product or service.
>
> **Function:** A work unit in an organization that provides a certain type of service or other output, e.g., accounting, distribution, planning, purchasing, or production.
>
> **Cross-functional process:** A process that occurs in more than one organizational function, department, or other major work unit.

For example, when one Naval shipyard's managers used activity mapping to improve their job order planning process, they expected to see that most of the work was done in the planning department. Instead, they found that at least half of it occurred outside that department. "Our thinking was stuck inside department and functional silos," said one manager. "This meant we were more concerned about efficiencies in individual work units, instead of the effectiveness of a whole process. Because of this, we might make a so-called 'improvement' in one department, but discover later that it caused problems somewhere else in the organization. With cross-functional process thinking we were able to see the full stream of work as it passed through all the parts of our organization. Without seeing that stream, how could we streamline?"

From this experience, we create a new management principle that states: *"When improving processes and activities, think and act across functional and departmental boundaries."* Taking this type of activity management one step further, organizations like the IRS have opted to organize their operations around cross-functional processes, rather than departments and functions.

Figure 1-5
Functional Silos
versus Cross-functional Processes

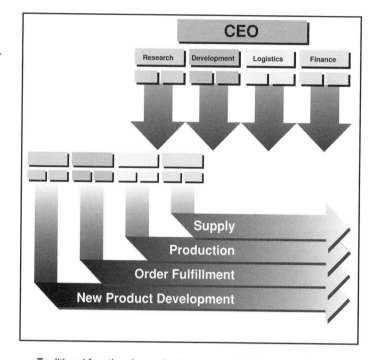

Traditional functional organizations are vertically managed and convenient for internal control. However, these functional structures often become "silos," major barriers to open communication and innovation.

Another major problem with most quality and reengineering approaches is that they lack adequate information on process performance and costs. Phillip Crosby's claim that "quality is free" is true only if you first understand what things cost and the benefit created by investing time and money improving them. Most public managers have no useful information about cost, nor can government accountants give it to them. Many quality initiatives founder and fail because they cannot present hard data to prove their worth. An ideal information system for quality management would include time, cost, quality, and customer satisfaction data related to how processes operate and what they produce. It would also allow managers to set priorities when they select processes to improve and measure the results of improvement. For example, Figure 1-6 compares an IRS center's traditional line-item budget to the same information presented in an ABC report format. If you wanted to make this center more cost effective, what information would the traditional budget provide to show you where to start? With the ABC information, you can readily see that "document and data presentation" is the most costly activity—a logical place to look for major cost reduction opportunities.

A final principle, then, is: *"Major process improvement depends on managers having accurate financial information on their processes."*

Traditional Line Items		New Way: Activity-Based Costing	
Salaries	$500,000	Prepare work plans	$30,000
Telecommuni-cations	100,000	Facilities and personnel planning	30,000
Enforcement expenses	50,000	Mail receipt and sorting	50,000
Facilities	30,000	Document and data preparation	180,000
Travel	20,000	Data entry	40,000
		Document and security control	130,000
		Data reconciliation	90,000
		Taxpayer file maintenance	110,000
		Refund requests/ correspondence	40,000
Total	$700,000	Total	$700,000

Figure 1-6
Traditional versus Activity Views of Costs
IRS Cincinnati Service Center – Processing Division

The Many Uses of Activity Costing and Management

You just read about a few of the uses of activity costing and management. There are many others, as you can see in Figure 1-7. In the rest of this book we will explore those that are most important to managers who want to create their own new principles of public administration. Now we will show you the types of private and public organizations that are currently doing this with activity costing and management.

Figure 1-7
Activity Costing
and Management
Areas of Analysis
and Reporting

Operating Results Outlook

- Activity budgeting
- Revenue and earnings results
- Summary of process-based operating results
- Causes for variation from budget/forecast
- Monitoring corrective action programs

Capital Expenditures

- Economic, non-economic justification (decision analysis)
- Project performance (including as benchmarked against other operations), in cost, service results, cycle time, and cost of quality (COQ)

Money Order Product/Service Costs

- Quantity of units delivered by activity, process, department, function, or activity center to internal or external customers
- Unit price (selling price, fee, transfer payment dollar value)
- Unit cost by unit/batch/product/facility and other levels
- Unit gross margins
- Comparison with prior year(s)/quarters(s)/ accounting period(s)

Performance Measurements

- Performance measures for cost, service results, cycle time, and COQ
- Cost and activity drivers of resource use by activities
- Control objectives (operational, functional, compliance) by activity

Accounting

- Collectability of past due accounts receivables
- Accounts payable

Marketing

- Cost of serving individuals or groups of customers
- Costs and causes of returns and allowances by product/service

Figure 1-7 (cont.)
Activity Costing
and Management
Areas of Analysis
and Reporting

Who Uses Activity Costing and Management?

In private industry, hundreds of companies have adopted the activity approach to cost finding and cost accounting. These range from manufacturers such as John Deere to service firms such as American Express. Many have gone a step further and adopted the activity management approach, such as Johnson & Johnson. The popularity of these approaches, especially ABC, is growing.

Well-known local government users include the City of Phoenix, Arizona, and the City of Indianapolis, Indiana. One of the federal government's largest employers, the U.S. Postal Service, is applying ABC to develop full cost and process improvement information for some of its major activities. Another public giant, IRS, has reorganized itself based on activity management principles, while its parent, the Treasury Department, is starting to use ABC. Defense Department users include the Navy's shipyards, the Air Force Space and Missile Systems Center, and the Defense Mapping Agency.

With increased emphasis on cost-effective government, more and more agencies will start to use ABC and to follow the principles of Activity-Based Management. That's because, as you will see in the next chapter, both provide the information and framework needed to successfully manage processes and their improvement.

Summary

Most governments have budgetary, accounting, and management systems that prevent them from seeing, much less acting on, opportunities to improve. One observer calls these systems "rat calculus": systems that have become such a parody of their original intent that the techniques of running through their self-created mazes are more important and interesting than asking whether the mazes do any good.[5]

Ironically, everyone knows this. For decades, they've also thought that most attempts to reform government simply rearrange the mazes — and they are being realistic, not cynical.

Right now, however, there's an opportunity to end rat calculus. The fiscal outlook for government is so grim and citizens are so angry that elected officials are anxious to tear down the walls so they won't be lined up in front of them.

ABC and Activity-Based Management offer a way to tear down those walls and empower public managers and employees to take the lead in reforming and reinventing government.

New Principles from Chapter 1

Meeting New Challenges With New Principles

Please use these two pages to develop your own new set of public management principles. To get you started, the new principles we suggested in this chapter are in the right column. Take a moment and write down their corresponding old rules or practices in the left column. We did the first two as examples.

Old Rule or Practice	New Principle or Practice
Use across-the-board budget and staff cuts to reduce costs.	Find and eliminate or reduce resources devoted to non-value added activity.
Overhead allocation masks the true costs of operations and is seldom questioned.	Know what activities, products, and services really cost, and understand what drives that cost.
	Know how your activities relate to each other and how they create and fulfill demands.
	Understand how your activities work now and how you want them to work in the future, before introducing new technology.
	Think and act across functional and departmental boundaries when improving processes and activities.
	Recognize that major process improvement depends on managers having accurate financial information about their processes.

· Old Rule or Practice	New Principle or Practice

Chapter

2

Management's Dysfunctional Thinking About Costs

- Most managers have no idea what their products and services really cost. At best, conventional cost accounting is marginally relevant to decisions about operations and improvement. At worst, it distorts reality and causes dysfunctional decisions.

- Governments try to make up for this problem by creating huge volumes of rules and regulations about spending.

- Activity-based costing developed from managers' need for realistic information on the cost of products, processes, and serving different groups of customers.

- With accurate information on costs and relationships among activities, managers make better decisions about product and service design and improvement and need fewer rigid rules on spending.

- Activity-Based Management restructures operations around processes and activities, practices top-down improvement, uses activity-based budgets, and creates flexible capacity.

"Management isn't about guessing, it's about knowing. Those in positions of responsibility must have the information they need to make good decisions. Good managers have the right information at their fingertips. Poor managers don't."

—From *Red Tape to Results: Creating a Government That Works Better and Costs Less*, Report of the National Performance Review

Information Should Influence Decisions

More than anything else, activity costing and management is about providing people inside an organization with accurate, relevant information to guide them in making the right decisions. This requires that people have accurate, timely information on costs, quality, speed, and customer expectations.

Unfortunately, right now most managers in both the public and private sectors have, at best, distorted information for making decisions, and many of their decisions are dysfunctional. This is especially true of information on cost and benefit:

- *Cost:* The total amount of resources, measured in dollars, spent to make a product or deliver a service.

- *Benefit:* The worth to customers, usually measured in dollars, of an activity, process, product, or service.

In the private sector, benefit is equivalent to market price, which usually is cost plus profit. Most of the time taxpayers do not expect public sector services to make a profit, but they always want the value of services to at least equal the cost.

Activity costing underscores the relationship between spending and the benefit that spending creates. In this chapter, you will see why this is a positive influence on management behavior.

Dollars Versus Bodies, "Free" Goods, and the $450 Hammer

The first book to outline the fundamental principles of ABC costing was *Relevance Lost: The Rise and Fall of Management Accounting*, which was written by H. Thomas Johnson and Robert S. Kaplan in 1985. The title is apt because much of what is called "cost accounting" is largely irrelevant to managerial decision-making.

The following examples show how poor cost accounting influences management behavior.

Dollars versus bodies. In most government agencies, the single most important budgetary item is the number of "full-time equivalents" (FTEs) allowed in a work unit. Managers strive to get more FTEs, while legislators alternate between cutting this head count and demanding more bodies for their pet programs. Often, neither managers nor lawmakers understand the waste this can cause.

> **Full-time equivalent (FTE)**: A measure of labor hours, e.g., two people who work half-time at a task make one FTE.

Dr. Dale R. Geiger studied the effect of cost awareness at IRS district offices.[6] In the study he found that managers responsible for these multimillion dollar organizations greatly underestimated the dollar cost of their staffs' salaries and wages, which was 85 percent of their budgets, because they were never asked to consider dollar costs. Instead, their orders were to keep the head count, or number of FTEs, within the budgeted limit.

The problem is that under this rule, $18,000-per-year employees cost a manager as much as $55,000-per-year employees because each represents one FTE in the budget. There was no incentive for managers to learn their employees' salaries and ask if the cost of this class of employee at least equals the benefits that employee class creates.

In the course of an ABC pilot project, the managers discovered that there were definite mismatches between employee salaries and the jobs they did. Highly paid professionals were doing standard, routine work better suited to paraprofessionals and even clerks. Now that they are armed with full information on costs, many of the managers are moving toward using more paraprofessionals and fewer professionals.

A variation of the "dollars versus bodies" problem is found in many military depots that make or repair weapons systems for Department of Defense customers. These depots calculate labor costs as standard "man-hour" or "man-day" rates, such as a $400 daily charge for each person working on a project. The same rate is used for unskilled laborers as for skilled artisans, so there is no incentive to reduce costs by shifting more work to less costly employees.

Closer to home, administrative budget cuts have probably just about wiped out your clerical staff. This happened at the IRS, and it means that supervisors and professionals spend much of their day typing, filing, and making copies. Activity costing would help reveal this waste and make a reasonable, practical case for more clerical support.

Hidden costs. Managers are often unaware of the true cost of their decisions. In a Texas chemical plant, supervisors did not mind having maintenance employees work overtime, because the $48-per-hour overtime cost (wages, fringe benefits, and overhead) charged to their accounts was not that much more than straight-time charges of $41 per hour. Activity costing showed the hidden costs of overtime: paperwork, supervision, support services, replacement workers, extra utilities, and others. The true cost of overtime turned out to be $55 per hour, versus the $34-per-hour true cost of straight time. In the three months after the analysis, the plant reduced overtime by about 40 percent.[7]

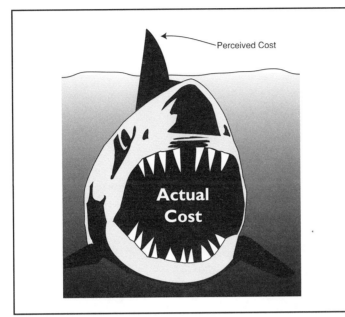

Figure 2-1
Perceived Versus
Actual Cost

Traditional cost accounting hides the actual cost of a product or service.

Hidden costs can also lead to the wrong decision about outsourcing or contracting out for government services. For example, to save money an agency decides to close its computer department and buy these services instead. The decision-makers may not realize that the total cost of the existing department probably cannot be contracted out, because some level of in-house supervision and coordination must remain. Added to this will be new costs for activities like writing requests for proposals, evaluating bids, and monitoring contracts. Failure to consider these costs means that the agency may be worse off financially with an outside contractor.

One cost triggers many others. Having accurate cost information during product, service, and process design is critical.

Up to 90 percent of total life cycle cost may be "locked in" at this phase. Knowing the downstream costs that early decisions will trigger makes people carefully consider their choices.

Some of the earliest activity cost systems were set up to influence the decisions of engineers as they designed new products and processes. For example, engineers might view their decision to make a new engineering drawing as costing only $95 for drafting. However, each new drawing triggered indirect activities such as inspection ($15), data processing ($25), quality control ($80), keeping stock ($20), and ordering parts ($40), for a total cost of $275. These downstream costs were not traced back to the original drawing.[8] When the engineers have full cost information, they will be more open to reusing an existing drawing instead of creating a new one.

Also, cost accounting systems that capture downstream costs make visible the benefits of using fewer components and more off-the-shelf parts in product design,[9] a plus for defense, energy, and aerospace agencies that buy or make ultrasophisticated products with high price tags. In software development, such accounting encourages reusing existing codes, which saves time and money used in quality control and debugging.

Finally, as we said in Chapter 1, activity costing removes the unrealistically high overhead rate often levied on direct labor. This allows a rational choice between using manual or automated activities and work steps.

Motivating improvement. Like every municipality, the City of Phoenix, Arizona, charges fees for permits, inspections, and licenses. The customers for these services range from real estate developers to dog owners. In 1980, however, activity cost analysis showed that fees the City collected were only about 40 percent of the costs of issuing them and providing related services. "In effect, taxpayers were subsidizing the people who received these services," said the

Phoenix city auditor in an interview for this book.

Before 1980, appropriations supported the City offices that provided user fee services. "With appropriations, you are better set up to absorb things like higher overhead costs, so you don't think too much about them," said the city auditor. "There's not as strong a motivation to look for cost savings, because you do not need them to survive."

Shocked by the information of the activity cost analysis, the Phoenix City Council issued a new policy of full cost recovery for user fees. Going further, the Council decided that the offices that provided user fee services had to be supported by the fees, not by appropriations.

Managers had two ways to go: fee adjustments and process improvement. For many, charging higher fees was not an option, because of pressure from user groups. To reduce costs through improvements, these managers were able to use process mapping information developed along with activity costs.

One example of improvement was in the process for planning plats for new real estate developments. Analysis of the process found that the City's aviation department (which runs the Phoenix airport) was always included, although it seldom really needed to be. By making this step optional, the city saved money, and plans were approved faster for service users.

As a result of improvements and fee adjustments, Phoenix now recovers almost all of the costs of its user fee services. "Another result is that the managers are much more sensitive about costs," said the city auditor. "For example, now that they're fee-supported, they cannot easily absorb increased overhead costs. They go over their overhead cost rates very carefully, and question them. They'll say to a city support or administrative department, 'Do you really have to do that?' That's a key question in the improvement process, one that the user fee offices are continually asked by their customers. It changes the way you think about your business."

Figure 2-2
The $450 Hammer

Accounting practices that distorted reality left the buying agency
open to career-busting criticism.

The $450 hammer revisited. Misleading cost accounting
information can itself trigger an agency's worst nightmare:
scandal, followed by legislators micromanaging operations
and adding still more walls to the mazes. Take the $450
hammer, for example. For those of you who don't remember
that infamous tool, here's what happened.

In the early 1980s, a defense agency bought an electronic
device (let's call it a "black box") along with a tool kit for it.
The invoice equally allocated the contractor's overhead
costs to each line item in this purchase. The $20,000 black
box cost $445 in overhead, *and so did each tool in the tool box,
including a $5 hammer!* Misunderstanding the numbers, a
technician outraged by this "procurement waste" reported it
up the chain of command. Along the way, someone leaked
the information to the media, which had a field day reporting on the so-called $450 hammer.

Defense officials argued in vain that the hammer did not
really cost $450. But it was true, according to accounting
rules. No one pointed out that, by the same rules, $445 in
overhead for the $20,000 black box was a bargain.

The $450 hammer story helped trigger investigations of

alleged fraud, waste, and abuse in the military procurement system. Despite finding few real problems, Congress wrote reams of new procurement regulations to solve them.

Now, neither you nor we are naive enough to think that the media and Congress failed to understand how that hammer really was priced. Still, accounting rules that distorted reality left the agency a casualty of career-busting criticism. The lesson to be learned from this: how you count money has to be rational and crystal clear to everyone inside and outside your organization.

Fig 2-3
Indirect Costs
Under Traditional
Accounting

Overhead/Indirect Costs: Traditional accounting spreads indirect/overhead costs evenly across direct costs— just like peanut butter. This is misleading because different activities consume different amounts of indirect costs.

Peanut butter rules. In the case of the $450 hammer, these were what we call "peanut butter" rules, because, like a peanut butter sandwich, they evenly spread overhead to every item and activity according to some allocation formula. Consider how such rules distort a "make or buy" decision in an agency: the in-house group that could provide the service or product may have its budget burdened with excessive overhead or administrative support that it seldom needs or uses. This can give an outside contractor a price advantage. The reverse can be true: the in-house group is at an unfair price advantage if it consumes a disproportionate amount of overhead, but this never shows up on the books because total indirect costs are spread evenly among all departments.

In the examples above, cost information played an important part in influencing management and stakeholder behavior. For the rest of this chapter, we will discuss why most accounting systems rarely give managers the economic information they need to make effective decisions.

Understanding this is particularly important for government policy-makers, Dr. Geiger told us in an interview. "Free goods have infinite demand, if you go strictly by an economic model. Most resources may seem 'free' to managers, if they do not know what they cost. But instead of introducing cost information and allowing managers to make rational economic decisions based on it, organizations make rules and guidelines on spending, like the 'head count' rule, procurement regulations, and others." In this next section, you'll find out how this came to be.

Cost Accounting and Cost Systems

ABC started out as a cost-finding branch of cost accounting, which is defined as "a branch of management accounting that clarifies, summarizes, measures, accumulates, controls, and reports on current or predicted costs, especially those of production."[10] Because cost-finding systems trace costs and revenues to the specific managers responsible for them, they are (or should be) one of the most powerful influences on managerial decision-making.

Traditional costing systems

Businesses developed what we call traditional, pre-ABC cost systems in the first half of the 20th century, when most had relatively undifferentiated products and services. Resources used to produce these outputs consisted mainly of direct labor and materials. Indirect or overhead expenses, such as sales departments and administrative and support services, were only a small percentage of total costs. Costs were accumulated and reported in cost centers that belonged to a single line, support department, or business unit.

Indirect costs were allocated to products or cost centers as an addition to direct labor or machine use hours. For example:

- If indirect costs were forecast to be $100,000 during a year, and

- 50,000 hours of direct labor were forecast, then

- Each direct labor hour worked was assigned $2 of indirect cost ($100,000/50,000 hours).

This system worked well enough until after World War II. Then, many businesses expanded their lines of products and services, and made technology and other changes that increased the overhead percentage of total costs. In manufacturing and some services, direct labor became a small part of total costs while overhead mushroomed. This caused serious distortions in traditional cost reports, because some products consumed much less overhead than others, yet were assigned the same overhead costs.

The man-day rate we discussed earlier is a good example of this distortion. For many government organizations and their contractors the actual salaries and benefits of line employees make up less than half of the total daily rate charged for them. The rest is indirect or overhead cost, mostly for the salaries and benefits of support and administrative employees. This is one reason most industrial companies have abandoned the standard man-day rate for more precise cost estimating and reporting.

Misleading measurement of the "push" production systems found in most factories also caused distortions. In push systems, products are made in long, uninterrupted production runs in anticipation of future sales. For example, some organizations allocated indirect costs by assigning "X" amount of overhead to each hour a machine was run. This often tempted managers to make more product units on these machines than a company could sell in the short term. Why? Because it lowered the overhead cost per unit, which in turn lowered total unit cost, which made the managers' numbers look more efficient. Unfortunately, this often became excess inventory that was "pushed" into warehouses, where it sat unsold.

Traditional cost accounting as the enemy of productivity

These and other problems caused line operation managers to doubt the information delivered by traditional cost systems. In the extreme, advocates of advanced production approaches called cost accounting "the number one enemy of productivity."[11] These approaches are often penalized by traditional cost systems because their short production runs appear inefficient. Dr. Taichi Ohno of Toyota, pioneer of the Just-In-Time (JIT) approach, once said, "I not only kept the cost accountants out of my plants; I tried to keep the knowledge of cost accounting principles out of the minds of my people."

> **Just-In-Time**: An approach to managing production that is designed to manufacture just the amount of product that is immediately required by customers. The "Big Three" auto makers all use the "JIT" approach.

Activity-Based Costing Emerges

In a strict sense, ABC is a set of costing tools and techniques. Some of the set were first applied in the 1960s at General Electric (GE), where they were called "activity cost analysis." GE's controllers noted that most indirect costs were triggered by upstream decisions made long before those costs were incurred. Our earlier example of the engineering drawings illustrates this. When these costs became visible to engineers, they started making more cost-effective decisions about product design.

In the 1970s and 1980s, ABC techniques emerged as a way of finding accurate cost data used to evaluate pricing. Again, it does this primarily by tracking indirect costs to the activities that produce specific products and services. This overcame the problem of allocating such costs by labor or machine hour. By applying ABC, many companies discovered that products thought to be highly profitable actually lost money, when all their overhead costs were considered. Later ABC analysis indicated which classes of customers were most profitable, and which actually consumed resources in excess of the revenues they generated.

ABC Used With Process Management

In the late 1980s and early 1990s, many organizations began to change their business philosophies to process-oriented approaches. Total Quality Management (TQM) is perhaps the best known of these. TQM emphasizes managing processes, or the way work is done, whereas older approaches focused on postproduction inspection, individual or work unit performance, budget variances, or simple efficiency. As organizations gained experience in TQM and ABC, many found that the two were highly compatible. ABC also focused on processes and provided information on how processes worked as well as on their cost and efficiency.

Process management approaches found uses for ABC beyond simply tracking costs and pricing studies. These included tools and data to assist in continuous improvement, benchmarking, cost-of-quality analysis, cycle time reduction, and business process reengineering. We discuss these in detail in the next chapter.

ABC is simply a set of valuable tools and techniques. It produces information for management decisions, but offers no operating philosophy to guide them. Activity-Based Management is such a philosophy.

Activity-Based Management Today

Recently, some organizations have made major modifications in their process management approaches to create what is called Activity-Based Management. In addition to ABC, the business practices of Activity-Based Management include those listed below. We discuss them in more detail in Chapter 8.

Figure 2-4
Characteristics of
Activity-Based
Management

- Activity-based costing

- Management structure built around core business processes

- Top-down and bottom-up emphasis on improvement

- Activity budgeting

- "Sizing" capacity to match work load

- Usually, the principles and practices of quality management

Management structure built around core business processes. A core business process is a series of linked line operations whose performance is critical to an organization's mission and survival. They transcend the functions and departments that control an organization's resources. Most organizations that practice cross-functional management depend on department and function chiefs to reach consensus on improvement and resource use.

In Activity-Based Management, process or activity owners manage the operations of business processes. Sometimes, these are line managers in charge of products, programs, and core business processes. At other times, they are the heads of the departments most concerned with a particular process, even though parts of that process fall outside their boundaries.

Process owners are in charge of operating, controlling, and improving their assigned processes. They have the authority to command resources from functions and departments, which are viewed as repositories for trained managers and employees needed to execute a process. Although consensus is desirable, it is clear and enforced that process owners are the customers of departments.

Top-down and bottom-up emphasis on improvement. By design or default, many new process improvement approaches focus only on bottom-up improvement. This means that middle managers and employees improve what they think is important, because top management neither has nor communicates strategic goals and objectives that should guide all improvement decisions.

In Activity-Based Management, corporate strategy sets the primary targets for improvement. Top management makes these targets a priority for all parts of the organization by communicating organizational goals and objectives and tracking improvement efforts aimed at achieving them. This is true top-down improvement. Middle managers and employees are still allowed to make other, less strategic improvements, because that is essential for true empowerment. Once everyone in the organization understands corporate strategy, however, they tend to focus on enhancing strategically important processes, products, and services. In this manner, bottom-up improvements are encouraged, but not at the expense of strategic investments.

Activity budgeting. Most organizations use line-item budgets to plan and control expenditures. Line items typically are arrayed by department under headings such as direct labor, direct materials, training, travel, facilities, and overhead.

In government and many businesses, line-item budgets are the primary tool top management uses for financial planning and controlling spending. Unfortunately, they also use these budgets to micromanage operations. The budgets are almost always, inadequate for measuring performance, because they rarely include measures of cost per process output.

If conditions are stable over time, such budgets become roughly congruent with operations, but when work load or funding changes quickly, using line-item budgets to change operations is clumsy, inadequate, and dangerous. They are used anyway, in a meat-ax way that scares people into writing resumes instead of finding ways to cut costs and meet new demands.

Organizations that use Activity-Based Management know they must maintain this traditional budget structure for external reporting. However, for internal planning and accountability, they develop an activity-based budget, with dollar amounts assigned to specific activities regardless of line item, based on the expected volume of output. Such budgets include targeted unit costs and quantities and appropriate performance measures. Managers have more discretion in how they spend their activity budget than they would using traditional budgeting methods. They are therefore better able to adjust to new demand and resource changes through the methods discussed below.

"Sizing" capacity to match work load. ABC's ability to identify and quantify resources devoted to line and support processes allows an organization to adjust capacity to variations in production demand. Before, such "sizing" often was a matter of guess work, especially in overhead departments. Thus, organizations that practice Activity-Based Management are able to treat capacity as a strategic variable instead of a fixed asset.

Quality management principles and practices. Organizations that follow Activity-Based Management usually also practice quality principles such as customer focus and employee empowerment. It is the practices listed above, however, integrated with the use of ABC tools and techniques, that set them apart from others.

Summary

In the past, managers' decisions often were not—indeed, could not be—in the best interest of their customers or their organizations because they had the wrong economic and customer value information. What is frightening is that few executives knew that their managers were wrong! Thus, the "rules of the game" set forth by executives and cost accountants required managers to behave in ways that suboptimized return on investment in improvement.

Activity-based costing gives managers more accurate feedback about costs and shows them the interrelationship of activities. This influences their behavior, which is guided by the principles and practices of Activity-Based Management.

New Principles from Chapter 2

Management's Dysfunctional Thinking About Costs

Because you are still new at this, we'll list two old rules; you put down the new principles. Then, you finish the rest of the list.

Old Rule or Practice	New Principle or Practice
Budgets have nothing to do with the reality of daily operations.	
Downstream costs are invisible in your cost estimates and budget, so why care about them?	

Old Rule or Practice	New Principle or Practice

Chapter

3

Linking Into Improvement Methods

- Activity costing and management are wholly compatible with other process management methods, and in fact are needed to complete them.

- During implementation of improvements, activity cost data help set priorities, while some ABC tools and methods are useful in determining what to change.

- Activity-based costing data help to measure the degree of success achieved in an improvement project, which helps customers, suppliers, management, and employees understand the value of continuous improvement.

"[T]he accounting systems of today have as much to do with inhibiting progress as any other factor. They're measuring efficiency in a world where effectiveness and quality are the key measurements."

—Robert K. Shank, "The Emerging
Revolution"

Most federal and many state and local government organizations have or are attempting to introduce new management methods and approaches. These include Total Quality Management (TQM), time-based management (TBM), and Just-In-Time (JIT). Recently, business process redesign or reengineering (BPR), which is used to radically change processes, has been added to the list.

Applied correctly, these approaches are powerful, so why do they need to be augmented with activity management and costing? Earlier, we gave two reasons:

- Most traditional accounting systems are, at best, marginally relevant to management decision-making, often misleading, and a barrier to informed decisions.

- Usually, they are structured around organizational units such as departments instead of process, which transcend departmental boundaries. In other words, they ignore or downplay cross-functional relationships.

Let us examine these reasons before going on to describe how activity costing and management combine with the three other approaches popular with government: TQM, TBM, and BPR.

Relevance of Cost Information to Process Improvement

Some quality "purists" argue that cost information is not very valuable when pursuing improvement. Their reasoning is that improvement comes from changing processes, reducing variation, training, and other actions from which cost savings will automatically follow. Is this true? The answer is yes and no.

Yes. Certainly, a myopic preoccupation with cost will doom any organization by drawing attention away from two critical aspects of process improvement. The first is customer expectations, which should be the "big gorilla" when it comes to making improvement decisions. The second is that not all improvements are "free." Many require heavy investment in technology and reengineering. Avoiding these costs simply to hold down expenses is the start of a "death spiral" for any organization.

Also, measures of factors that drive costs are more useful than cost data itself at the operations level. These include statistics on variation, cycle time, and error rates. Finally, few or no systems of cost information can provide rapid feedback on performance, so they have little value for short-term process control. Activity costing can help build those measures, but cannot deliver them quickly by itself.

> In this world, nothing takes care of itself, including cost. Lowering costs must be a process improvement objective—not the only one, and often not the most important—but it must be there, clearly stated.

No. According to Robert S. Kaplan, one of the codifiers of activity-based costing, "The idea that costs will take care of themselves if managers focus on improving quality. . . makes one wonder how some Malcolm Baldrige Award winners encountered severe financial difficulties."[12] He points out that improving a process does not automatically result in lower cost or higher revenue. Too often, process improvement creates unused capacity that remains in the process, so there is no cost savings. Equally often, improvements focus on services that customers do not value.

Right now, cost savings is a primary survival goal of most businesses and all governments. Make no mistake: with tight home budgets, consumers today shop for price. With tight public budgets, so do governments. Costs count, and must be counted when making process improvements. Quality improvement is not free: its benefits must exceed costs.

Understanding the Relationship of Activities

Again, "purists" will say—and rightly—that their approaches recognize the need to understand the relationship of all activities. However, the manner in which TQM, TBM, and BPR most commonly have been applied in government largely ignores cross-functional relationships. In Chapter 1, you saw an example of lack of understanding of those relationships: the shipyard job order planning process, half of which took place outside the planning department. Here we look at the same problem in an entire organization: the U.S. Internal Revenue Service (IRS).

The IRS is among the oldest and most advanced users of TQM in the federal government. Several of its units have won the Quality Improvement Prototype award, a high honor in federal quality. One has won the President's Award for Quality, the highest honor. No one can deny that in the last half-decade the productivity and quality of IRS services have increased greatly.

Yet, according to one senior IRS manager, "Ours was a bottom-up quality approach, which was good for involving local employees in making improvements and has saved millions of dollars. But this approach 'hit the wall' when it came to working on cross-functional processes, those that involve many departments and the entire IRS organization."

He continues, "This should come as no surprise: functions and departments are by nature introspective. They communicate well internally, but shut the door on outside inputs, which they think are 'crazy.' We wanted to get past that barrier and start doing top-down improvement as well as bottom-up. That's why we started organizing around what we

call core business systems made up of cross-functional processes."

Most executives and managers have blinders on when it
comes to improvement. These blinders are the boundaries of
their departments and divisions—what happens beyond the
boundaries is unknown and unimportant. In process terms,
they do not clearly see the relationship of the activities that
they directly control to other activities in their organizations.
They decide in isolation to improve activities, so they often
achieve suboptimal gains.

Activity-Based Management begins with the idea that organizations have only a few truly important major cross-functional processes. The IRS has organized these into core
business systems, such as the five shown in Figure 3-1, that
encompass all IRS operations. One of the first jobs is to identify these major processes and systems, which provide a
framework of activity relationships for making improvements. This way you make decisions with full understanding of outcomes, up and down a cross-functional chain of
activities.

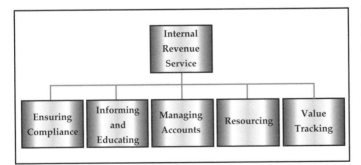

Figure 3-1
IRS Core Business
Systems

This increases the likelihood of optimizing return on investments in improvement and forces a new way of thinking
that is healthier for an organization. This is the horizontal
view of cross-functional processes as opposed to the vertical
view of functional "silos" shown in Figure 1-5.

In summary, cost information and cross-functional thinking often are missing from most process-oriented improvement approaches. With this in mind, let us now examine how activity costing and management integrate with and improve these approaches.

Quality Management

TQM is a set of principles, tools, and procedures that guide the practical affairs of running an organization. TQM has become the leading new management approach in government. In 1992, about 68 percent of federal organizations had quality initiatives.[13] Many state and local governments (including Arkansas, under the leadership of then-Governor Clinton) have done the same.

In their book *Excellence in Government: Total Quality Management in the 1990s*, David K. Carr and Ian D. Littman of Coopers & Lybrand define TQM as:

Involving everyone in an organization in controlling and continuously improving how work is done, in order to meet customers' expectations of quality.

According to Carr and Littman, quality means everything of value to a public service organization and its customers. This includes the physical quality of the products and services, productivity, efficiency, ethics, morale, safety, and wise use of resources.

Figure 3-2 shows TQM's distinguishing characteristics. Practitioners of Activity-Based Management often draw their customer focus emphasis from quality management and use many TQM tools and procedures. On the other hand, activity costing and management add to TQM by helping to measure results, set priorities, and manage improvement teams.

Traditional Management	Total Quality Management
Needs of users of products and services defined by specialists	Customer focus, where users of products and services define what they want
Errors and waste tolerated if they do not exceed set standards	No tolerance for errors, waste, and work that does not add value to products and services
Products and services inspected for problems, then "fixed"	Prevention of problems
Many decisions governed by assumptions and gut feelings	Fact-based decisions using hard data and scientific procedures
Short-term planning based around budget cycle	Long-term planning based on improving mission performance
Product or service designed sequentially by isolated departments	Simultaneous design of total product or service life cycle by teams from many functions
Control and improvement by individual managers and specialists	Teamwork among managers, specialists, employees, vendors, customers, and partner agencies
Improvement focused on one-time breakthroughs such as computers and automation	Continuous improvement of every aspect of how work is done
Vertical structure and centralization based on control	Horizontal and decentralized structure based on maximizing value added to products and services
Short-term contracts awarded based on price	Vendor partnership of long-term buyer/seller obligations, based on quality and continuous improvement

Figure 3-2
Traditional Versus
Total Quality
Management

Measuring results

Most government improvement programs have problems showing that they save money. This serious shortcoming is a ready reason for killing good quality initiatives. Activity costing provides the following:

- Baseline costs of "as is" processes and activities, before they are improved

- The data needed to test alternative process improvement solutions for their cost efficiency

- Actual (not speculated) cost savings from improvement projects.

Rewarding results

Accurate measurement of improvement is essential for paying bonuses and other rewards. For example, many TQM organizations pay bonuses to managers and employees who improve processes, and these rewards are often a percentage of cost savings gained. Another related system is gainsharing, the practice of dividing a portion of total annual savings among all employees. Although not the only reward that motivates improvement, money signals importance. Activity costing helps to figure out with some precision the amount of money saved, thus providing a baseline for bonuses and gainsharing.

Setting priorities

Too often, managers use the "squeaky wheel principle" to decide what to improve. In fact, decisions as to where to focus improvement resources should be based on customer expectations. When customers want improved quality and lower cost, activity costing and management show where to start.

Figure 3-3 shows an activity breakdown of a process that receives, stores, and distributes material in a Naval shipyard. Each activity is quantified by its labor cost, which is about 90 percent of all costs. Judging by costs alone, the greatest savings may come from improving these activities: receive material at dock ($95,000 per year) and inspect material ($76,000).

This is accurate cost information, but still not the whole picture. Figure 3-3 shows that value analysis, a tool of activity management, has been applied to these activities. Of the two highest cost activities, only "receive material at dock" adds value. Most non-value activities exist because of deficiencies in the system of operations. If there were no need to "inspect material," the process would move faster. Working with suppliers, this organization could improve the quality of materials to the point where they had zero defects. Thus, the logical place to start looking for improvement and maximum cost savings is "inspect material."

| Activity | FTE | $$ in 000's | |
		Total $$	Non-value Added $$
Receive material at dock	3.48	$95	0
Identify material	1.53	42	0
Store material (temporary)	2.09	57	57
Inventory warehouse	0.14	4	4
Segregate by delivery point	2.09	57	57
Load material for delivery	1.39	38	0
Inspect material	2.79	76	76
Clean up receiving area	0.42	11	11
Total	**13.93**	**$379**	**$205**

Figure 3-3
Shipyard Cost Model for Material Activities

Managing improvement teams

Most TQM organizations go through a phase in which their improvement teams run into major problems: the right people are not on the team; no one knows where a process begins or ends; there are no firm targets for improvement; and there is no way to measure the amount of improvement.

Activity mapping and analysis done at the outset help to define process boundaries. These steps also show who should be on a team: people from activities within the process. Activity costs provide financial baseline data and activity analysis determines cycle time. With this information management can set quantified objectives, which helps teams choose improvement approaches. Finally, activity costing helps quantify results.

Shifting top management from sloganeering to action

One of the major problems in introducing TQM and other process-oriented approaches is the top management's failure to support them. This is because these managers often do not understand the magnitude of quality problems. Activity costing methods dramatically quantify the potential savings of improvement.

For example, Figure 1-2 in Chapter 1 shows the total cost of non-value added activity in one government organization that "sells" its services to other government groups. Do you think customers would be upset that two-thirds of their money is going to support work that does not improve the services they buy? The answer has certainly been clear to the organization's executives, who now are quality enthusiasts.

Cost-of-quality analysis

Cost-of-quality analysis (COQ) is a tool of TQM. Also called the "cost of nonconformance," in COQ an organization identifies the amount of resources it devotes to four categories of non-value added activity:

- **Prevention:** The cost of preventing problems, rejects, errors, scrap, and waste. This may include training, some quality assurance functions, developing procedures,

TQM work, pre-award surveys, and other related costs. Sometimes, prevention is called the "cost of conformance" with customer expectations.

- **Appraisal:** The cost of inspecting for errors. In the shipyard example just given, the outside materials received were inspected. Inspection also may include laboratory tests, reviews, calibration, and maintaining inspection equipment, production audits, and customer acceptance inspections. Quality control falls under this category. In a white-collar operation, this would include the cost of reviewing all reports, budgets, estimates, contracts, letters, and all other documents for accuracy and fit.

- **Internal failure:** The costs of redoing work, discarding defects, delays owing to lack of some needed component or information, requests for specification deviations, and scrap and all other forms of waste that occur before a product or service is delivered to an internal or external customer.

- **External failure:** The cost of any repairs or rework done after you deliver a product or service to a customer. This includes rework done by the customer; investigations by oversight groups due to failures; answering complaints; and products, reports, or other items returned because they did not perform as intended.

COQ information helps you start shifting quality costs up the line until they occur mainly in the prevention category at greatly reduced levels. Working hard on COQ typically lowers it from 20 percent to 30 percent of all costs to less than 10 percent.

One of COQ's toughest problems is to develop accurate cost information, but ABC can readily resolve it. Figure 3-4 shows how process analysis followed by activity costing helped do this in a COQ assessment of a university's administrative and support departments. Extra benefits from using activity costing and management with COQ include the following:

- It associates the cost of nonconformance with specific activities within a process

- It captures all the costs associated with these activities, which shows the true cost of nonconformance

- It lends itself to additional research, such as value and cost driver analyses.

Figure 3-4
ABC and COQ in a
University

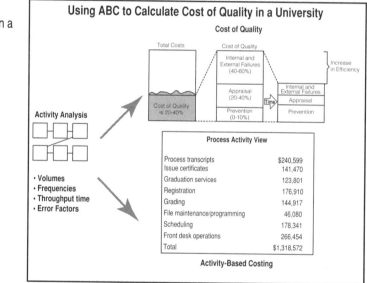

Using ABC to Calculate Cost of Quality in a University

Process Activity View	
Process transcripts	$240,599
Issue certificates	141,470
Graduation services	123,801
Registration	176,910
Grading	144,917
File maintenance/programming	46,080
Scheduling	178,341
Front desk operations	266,454
Total	$1,318,572

If you are doing activity costing anyway, it is easy to produce reports on COQ—simply code COQ activities by their respective categories. Usually, however, it is not cost-effective to use activity costing merely to produce COQ information, so you have to plan to use the activity costing information for other purposes as well. Most organizations initially can get enough COQ information with rough estimates.

Empowerment

Much has been said about the need to empower people to take control of their work processes. Perhaps the greatest contribution that activity management makes to empowerment is to help people understand the work they do. It does this by first showing the line supervisor and employee how they actually work and the place their work occupies in the "big picture." Second, it helps people identify what causes variation in work load—the activity and cost drivers discussed in Chapter 5—so that they can target their improvement efforts.

The third reason is explained by a financial accounting manager at Johnson & Johnson Medical, Inc.: "[Activity-Based Management] links the why and how of work to empowerment. The questioning of how work is done in financial accounting was unheard of years ago. Activity-Based Management has done away with the belief that if you don't do the same thing as before, your job will be in jeopardy. Now everyone in the [financial accounting] department feels free to challenge their work base. This is completely new."[14]

Time-Based Management

Time-Based Management (TBM) is one of several names for an improvement approach that focuses on reducing cycle time by eliminating waste. Cycle time is the amount of time it takes a unit of output to travel through a process from start to finish. For major cross-functional processes, time usually begins with a triggering event like a customer order or request, and ends when the order is filled.

TBM focuses on waste, which is defined as:

Anything other than the minimum amount of equipment, materials, parts, space, and worker's time that is absolutely essential to add value to the product.

This is one definition used in value analysis to define "non-value added." In TBM, an activity adds value to a product or service if it meets the following conditions:

- The customer recognizes the value

- It changes the product

- It is done right the first time.

Figure 3-5 Product Process Map

Type of Activity	No.	Total Time
Operations	9	10m
Transport	6	22m
Inspections	1	2m
Wait	4	26m
Storage		
Distance Traveled 8m + delivery		60m

Process: Pizza delivery

Map Begins: Order placed

Map Ends: Pizza delivered to customer

	Activities of the Product	Operation	Transport	Inspection	Wait	Storage	Distance	Time	Value added	Notes
1.	Order placed	✓						30s	✓	
2.	Wait for action				✓			2m		
3.	Dough shaped	✓						30s	✓	
4.	Dough spread into pie pan	✓						30s	✓	
5.	Pie crust shaped	✓						30s	✓	
6.	Sauce added	✓						30s	✓	
7.	Cheese added	✓						30s	✓	
8.	Toppings added	✓						30s	✓	
9.	Wait for baking				✓			8m		
10.	Placed in oven		✓				1	30s		
11.	Baked	✓						6m	✓	
12.	Removed from oven		✓				1	30s		
13.	Placed in box		✓				1	1m		
14.	Cut into slices	✓						30s	✓	
15.	Inspected for quality			✓				2m		
16.	Placed on hot rack		✓				3	2m		
17.	Wait for delivery				✓			5m		
18.	Placed in hot bag		✓				2	1m		
19.	Wait for transport				✓			1m		
20.	Transported to customer		✓				<6k	17m		

s = seconds   m = minutes   k = kilometers

TBM is favored by organizations to which speed is important. For example, AlliedSignal's TBM credo is, "We focus on speed for competitive advantage. We simplify processes and compress cycle time." By doing this, the Fortune 50 company can bring new products to market faster and respond better to customers and markets. As done at AlliedSignal, TBM often is used with TQM as one of many "vehicles" for the journey toward quality.

ABC methods are used in TBM to identify, describe, and sequence activities in a process. Having done this, you can then measure an activity's cycle time, and the "wait" or "queue" time that work-in-process spends between activities. Figure 3-5 shows how activity analysis is applied in TBM, using an example of pizza delivery from a Coopers & Lybrand's training exercise. Notice that the matrix in the figure records the time spent for each activity in the process. In addition, it lists five categories of activities using process engineering categories: operation, transport, inspection, wait, and storage. These are called activity attributes, and we will discuss them more in Chapter 4.

These categories are useful in many white-collar processes as well. For example, people may spend an hour working on a purchase order, but that same order may consume several weeks of cycle time in transport, inspection, and, most of all, waiting for the next activity to begin.

Several government organizations use TBM methods of looking at time information. Says one IRS manager, "Cycle time is one of our most important indicators of whether we are satisfying our customers. Taxpayers don't want to be put on hold on the phone for several minutes to get an answer to a tax question, and they want their refunds promptly. We've always measured cycle time, but with activity analysis we can better understand what drives time up or down."

Business Process Reengineering

BPR is a relatively new methodology for carrying out radical changes in organizations. Many of these changes are made possible by new technology, especially in the field of information systems. For example, the IRS has redesigned its process of filing 1040EZ forms from a paper operation to one in which taxpayers use touch-tone telephones to directly enter this information into IRS computers.

Coopers & Lybrand's approach is called BreakPoint BPR[SM] because it focuses on achieving strategic "breakpoints," or performance levels that ensure strong positive response from customers. Instead of applying improvement techniques to individual functions and their processes, BreakPoint BPR operates at an organization-wide level by identifying and working on broad, cross-functional processes.

Activity analysis

As discussed in Chapter 1, activity mapping and analysis should be basic BPR and information technology tools. A federally chartered financial institution discovered this while installing a major new information system as part of reengineering. In reviewing one cross-functional process scheduled for automation several years after the others, a team using activity mapping methods identified the critical links from that cross-functional process to those other processes. These links otherwise would have been missed, resulting in expensive reconfiguration of the information system after it was installed. Also, value analysis helped determine which activities should be eliminated in the new information system, instead of wasting money automating them.[15]

Process modeling and simulation

Activity mapping provides data needed for process modeling, an increasingly popular tool of BPR and new process design. Modern process modeling uses sophisticated simulation software to construct "as-is" process models that include work steps and resources consumed. Such models are easily manipulated, allowing "what-if" analysis on alternative process designs. According to a top IRS manager, "If you collect activity information, you're missing the boat unless you use it for process simulation modeling. We use such modeling extensively as a low-cost testing method for new process ideas."

Process simulation and modeling software comes in many varieties and sizes, including versions for personal and minicomputers. More important than the software, however, is basic understanding of process design, which activity analysis provides.

Economic analysis

Activity-based costing is essential in choosing processes for redesign. BPR is an expensive undertaking that sometimes requires millions of dollars in new technology, making accurate cost/benefit analysis a necessity. ABC can be used to determine the costs of several processes that are candidates for reengineering; then you can analyze their potential for improvement based on value added/non-value added (VA/NVA), COQ costs, and traditional cost/benefit calculations. Finally, activity costing during reengineering makes it possible to search for least-cost alternatives.

Measuring results

As with TQM, ABC allows you to measure the cost savings generated by a BPR project. This validates earlier cost/benefit calculations. More important you can continue to measure results over time, which is critical for continuous improvement.

Why is this last benefit so important? The answer is entropy: all processes have a natural tendency to become less efficient from the day they are installed. This may be due to small failures in various parts of the process, poor maintenance, or "creeping bureaucracy" that adds unnecessary steps and activities to the process. Also, customer requirements and expectations shift constantly, making what you produce today, and how you produce it, obsolete tomorrow. Regular review of customer expectations ensures that you are doing the right thing. Identifying cost or cycle time increases in various activities using activity costing and management methods helps to ensure you continue to do the process correctly.

Summary

Because activity costing and management are process-based, they are ideal companions for other process-based approaches such as TQM, TBM, and BPR. By adding cost information and forcing a process view of operations, activity costing and management help to solve many of the problems organizations encounter when using these other approaches.

New Principles from Chapter 3

Linking Into Improvement Methods

Now, you are on your own, but this time think about more than traditional management rules or practices. Also consider those of your organization's Total Quality Management, Time-Based Management, reengineering, or other process management initiatives. Put down their actual rules or practices—not the ones you may have learned in a training course or book, but those that are applied in your organization.

Old Rule or Practice	New Principle or Practice

Old Rule or Practice	New Principle or Practice

PART II

BUILDING BLOCKS OF
ACTIVITY-BASED
COSTING

Chapter

4

Activity Basics

- Activities are essential to develop, make, sell, deliver, or support an organization's products and services.

- Analyzing activities is key to understanding how resources are consumed, how costs are incurred, and how improving the ways in which activities are performed can affect the "bottom line."

- The level of activity-related detail managers need depends on what makes sense in their situation. Strategic planning efforts may require examining combinations of the activities performed in a few major cross-functional processes; specific operations efforts may require you to examine activities in much greater detail.

- Using storyboarding techniques and compiling activity dictionaries allow you to assemble the information you need to determine how your organization generates costs.

"A management system structured on activities ensures that plans are transmitted to a level at which action may be taken. Activities are what organizations do. To make changes, one must change what people or machines do. Therefore, changes must ultimately be made to activities."

—James A. Brimson and
John Antos

In this and the following two chapters, you will learn the basic methods and techniques of activity-based costing. In this chapter, we will focus on the first steps in using ABC information: developing an activity dictionary and activity maps or models of an organization.

The Activity Dictionary

An activity dictionary is a lexicon of the different activities performed in an organization. Its purpose is to define each activity so that everyone will understand and agree on what an activity means. Another name for such a dictionary is a chart of activities.

An activity dictionary lists activities in generic terms; organizes them by process, department, or function; and defines each activity and process. Sometimes an activity dictionary will include other information about an activity.

Activity dictionaries come in many forms. For example, Figure 4-1 shows a sample of the dictionary used by the U.S. Postal Service's Postal Money Order operation. Figure 4-2 is a page from a generic dictionary you can buy commercially (see Appendix A for more information on it). Note that it includes possible performance measures and other information about each activity, such as input, output, output measure, characteristics, and cost drivers. These are all useful for understanding, controlling, and improving activities, as you will see in this chapter.

Process 7.1: Perform money order general accounting, budget, treasury, and internal audit functions.

7.1.1: Receive and report on money order cost accounting data obtained from the general ledger/in-office cost system. Includes:
- Data acquisition and maintenance
- Data analysis
- General reporting of results

7.1.2: Perform money order general letter maintenance procedures and reporting. Includes:
- Perform monthly close
- Perform asset maintenance functions (systems, inventory, etc.)
- Internal and external reporting
- Manage and collect accounts receivable

7.1.3: Conduct all money order, treasury, and finance functions. Includes:
- Collect and disburse cash
- Determine investment strategy and maintain portfolio records (cash management)
- Identify and purchase insurance
- Perform financial analysis

7.1.4: Perform money order internal audit function. Includes:
- Insure financial accountability at issuing offices and accountable paper units
- Provide opinion on the money order system
- Conduct operations and controls review and propose recommendations
- Prepare special studies

Figure 4-1
U.S. Postal
Service Data
Dictionary
Money Order
Activity List

Figure 4-2
Generic Activity
Dictionary

ACTIVITY	Select Vendor
FUNCTION	Purchasing
PROCESS	Procurement Design and Development
ACTIVITY DEFINITION	The process of choosing vendors against defined criteria to supply necessary materials or services to the business
INPUTS	A request to select a supplier The supplier's performance data A bid A new product A proposal
OUTPUTS	A selected supplier
OUTPUT MEASURE	The number of suppliers selected
ACTIVITY CHARACTERISTICS	Primary Value added
COST DRIVERS	Policies and procedures Number of vendors Number of parts Quality of materials

Source: *Activity Dictionary*, see Appendix A.

Activities are active

Usually, the process and activity definitions in such a dictionary begin with a verb: "counsel employees," "verify documents," and "monitor contracts," for example. By underscoring the active nature of work, verbs help people develop a process-oriented rather than a "job description"-oriented perspective. Using commonly understood verbs and nouns forces people away from the technical jargon and acronyms that make it hard for others to understand what is done in an activity.

It is not necessary to start from scratch in developing your activity dictionary. Generic dictionaries like the one just mentioned offer some standard definitions as well as starting points for unique ones, but everyone with experience (including the authors of generic dictionaries) agrees on the need to customize definitions to the specific type of work done in your organization. For the rest of the chapter, you will learn how to do this.

Some Working Definitions

In this section, we'll do a quick overview of the basic terms of activity costing and management that you'll be learning to use throughout this book. Most of this will be familiar ground if you are experienced in using Total Quality Management.*

---

* There are slight differences between activity and TQM terminology. For example, "activity" as used here is the same as a simple process in quality management, while "process" here corresponds to a short series of linked simple processes within the same function or department.

The activity hierarchy

In activity costing there is a hierarchy of operations, illustrated by the pyramid in Figure 4-3. Each level is an aggregation of the ones below it. Executives make decisions about the highest level, such as what goals to set and where to make high-cost improvement investments. Managers and employees working in the lower levels contribute information and recommendations to guide decisions at the higher levels. They also determine how best to implement goals within their processes or activities.

Figure 4-3
The Activity
Pyramid

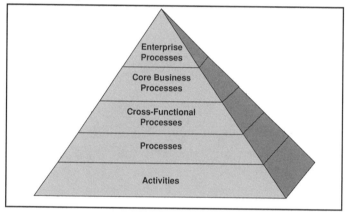

Activity. An *activity* is a unit of work usually done by one or more persons belonging to the same office, branch, or other small group. Examples include daily business activities such as paying bills, taking customer orders, or administering X-rays. Within an activity there are discrete *tasks*, such as preparing a patient for an X-ray, doing the X-ray, developing the film, or sending the film to a physician. Tasks are made up of even smaller units of work called *steps*, such as positioning an X-ray machine on the right part of a patient's body.

As shown in Figure 4-4, every activity has *inputs*: material and information from another source. Inside the activity, the inputs are *transformed* or converted into identifiable *outputs*: a product or service, and sometimes information on the output. The internal components of the transformation include the people who do the work in the activity; the equipment, methods, and supplies they use; and the physical environment where the activity exists.

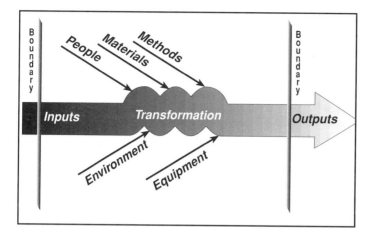

Figure 4-4
Components of an Activity

Activities have identifiable *boundaries*, or starting and ending points. They start when people inside the transformation component gain control over inputs, and stop when these same people hand over control of outputs to another activity, or to external customers.

All activities have *customers* and *suppliers*. An activity's internal customer is another activity inside the organization that receives output or information from the first activity. In this situation, the first activity is the supplier of the second activity. External customers are outside the organization, including scientists who receive grants (outputs) from a scientific agency; organizations that receive satellite photographs (outputs) from an intelligence agency; and citizens who receive family assistance (output) from a welfare agency.

External suppliers are people and organizations outside an agency that provide it with materials, information, or services. A company that sells asphalt (input) to a city road maintenance department is an external supplier. A citizen who provides information (input) on his or her financial status to a welfare agency is an external supplier of that information.

In process-oriented management approaches such as TQM and Activity-Based Management, improvement comes from changing one or more components of inputs, transformation, or outputs. For example, a better grade of asphalt (input) may improve the activity of repairing chuckholes or cracks in streets. A new maintenance schedule (a method component of transformation) may prevent breakdowns of equipment. Providing a report on computer disk (output) may make it more useful to customers than a printed document (output).

Process. Linked together in logical sequence and having identifiable boundaries, a group of activities form a process. The outputs of one activity become the inputs of the next, until a final process output is produced. For example, the process of qualifying people for public assistance might include the five activities of (1) collecting information from them (input); (2) reviewing the information to see if they qualify; (3) verifying the information; (4) reporting the names of eligible persons to another process that arranges for assistance (a final output of this process); and (5) notifying ineligible persons that they do not qualify (another final output).

Cross-functional process. When the activities of a process are done in several different functions or departments in an organization, this is called a *cross-functional process*. For example, Figure 4-1 shows a cross-functional process, "perform money order general accounting, budget, treasury, and internal audit functions." This process is carried out in activities done by several departments and functions and involves many functions. You are no doubt familiar with the cross-functional process of procurement, which involves: (1) a line department, where a need is recognized and reported (2) to a purchasing department that arranges to buy a product or service to fill the need and sends the seller's invoice (3) to an accounting or finance department that pays the bill.

There can be dozens and even hundreds of cross-functional processes in an organization, ranging from making the products and services customers value the most, to support operations such as arranging and paying for local travel expenses. One of the key objectives of ABC is to make these cross-functional processes visible to executives and managers. This enables an organization to introduce changes that will improve the entire cross-functional process, not just one or two of the activities or processes that are part of it.

Core business process. *A core or strategic business process* is a cross-functional process that is a "survive-or-die" operation. Failure to do this type of process correctly will jeopardize your organization's mission. These operations almost always directly produce the goods and services your external customers value the most. Some examples of core business processes include collecting revenues in a treasury department, recruiting qualified enlisted personnel for a defense organization, and preventing the outbreak of communicable disease by a health department. A few support processes, such as ensuring the safety of employees who handle explosives or nuclear fuels, qualify for this category.

Enterprise processes. For some government operations, these processes are at the top of the pyramid and flow through several independent or quasi-independent organizations. They are part of the *value chain* for some types of products and services. A value chain is a stream of processes, each of which adds value to a final product or service. In an enterprise process, the chain may begin with one organization acquiring raw material or data and supplying it to another that produces a part or component. The second organization supplies the part to a third that uses it to make and supply a final product or service to an end user customer. If needed, the third organization, or perhaps a fourth, provides ongoing support services to that customer.

For example, the life cycle of a weapons system is an enterprise process. Its value chain starts with recognizing a threat (a transformation of raw data into useful information); includes system development, deployment, and upgrades (transformations of information and raw materials into a product that is delivered to end user customers); and maintenance and eventual disposing of equipment and material (post-delivery service). Many Department of Defense and military service organizations—and even the U.S. Congress—may take part in this enterprise.

Whether you need to consider enterprise processes in your organization depends on the types of products and services you produce. If these products and services are essential to a larger, multi-organization operation, then the concepts of the enterprise process and the value chain are handy ways to understand where your organization fits in the "big picture." For elected officials, the concept provides perhaps the most accurate and revealing view of the big picture.

Figure 4-5 IRS Core Business Processes

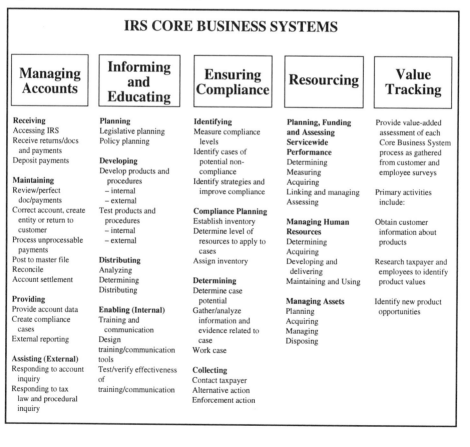

IRS CORE BUSINESS SYSTEMS

Managing Accounts	Informing and Educating	Ensuring Compliance	Resourcing	Value Tracking
Receiving	**Planning**	**Identifying**	**Planning, Funding**	Provide value-added
Accessing IRS	Legislative planning	Measure compliance	**and Assessing**	assessment of each
Receive returns/docs	Policy planning	levels	**Servicewide**	Core Business System
and payments		Identify cases of	**Performance**	process as gathered
Deposit payments	**Developing**	potential non-	Determining	from customer and
	Develop products and	compliance	Measuring	employee surveys
Maintaining	procedures	Identify strategies and	Acquiring	
Review/perfect	– internal	improve compliance	Linking and managing	Primary activities
doc/payments	– external		Assessing	include:
Correct account, create	Test products and	**Compliance Planning**		
entity or return to	procedures	Establish inventory	**Managing Human**	Obtain customer
customer	– internal	Determine level of	**Resources**	information about
Process unprocessable	– external	resources to apply to	Determining	products
payments		cases	Acquiring	
Post to master file	**Distributing**	Assign inventory	Developing and	Research taxpayer and
Reconcile	Analyzing		delivering	employees to identify
Account settlement	Determining	**Determining**	Maintaining and Using	product values
	Distributing	Determine case		
Providing		potential	**Managing Assets**	Identify new product
Provide account data	**Enabling (Internal)**	Gather/analyze	Planning	opportunities
Create compliance	Training and	information and	Acquiring	
cases	communication	evidence related to	Managing	
External reporting	Design	case	Disposing	
	training/communication	Work case		
Assisting (External)	tools			
Responding to account	Test/verify effectiveness	**Collecting**		
inquiry	of	Contact taxpayer		
Responding to tax	training/communication	Alternative action		
law and procedural		Enforcement action		
inquiry				

Figure 4-6 IRS' Ensuring Compliance Core Business Process

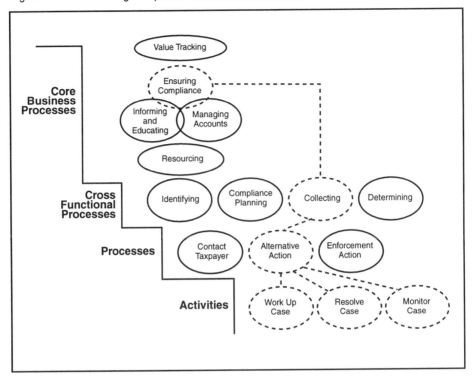

An example hierarchy: the IRS. Now, let's see how an activity pyramid works in real life, at the IRS. The chart in Figure 4-5 is a high-level *business model* of IRS operations. At the top are the five *core business processes* considered to be most important by the IRS: managing accounts, informing and educating taxpayers, ensuring compliance, resourcing, and value tracking. Let's spend a moment on them.

The major division chiefs at the IRS identified their five core business processes at the start of their Activity-Based Management initiative. Other organizations approach this from the opposite end of the pyramid, working upward from activities.

Look just below the IRS' core business processes in Figure 4-5, and you'll see several narrowly focused, but still cross-functional, processes. Another way of looking at them is shown in Figure 4-6, where the "ensuring compliance" core business process is broken down into four smaller, cross-functional processes: "identifying," "compliance planning," "determining," and "collecting."

"Collecting," in turn, is disaggregated into three smaller processes whose activities occur mostly in field offices. The IRS defines the three as follows:

- **Contact with Taxpayer.** This process has as its boundary those activities that begin when a taxpayer has a balance due, and ends either with full and immediate payment of the balance, or with referral to the Alternative Action or Enforcement Action processes.

- **Alternative Action.** This process begins when a taxpayer acknowledges that he or she will not pay the full balance due immediately. It ends when the taxpayer pays the balance due in full, or with case closure or referral to the Enforcement Action process.

- **Enforcement Action.** This process begins when a balance due cannot be resolved through Alternative Action and ends with full payment, case closure, or when the taxpayer proceeds with an Alternative Action.

Each process has products or cost objects. For example, Alternative Action has several: full payment of the balance due; installment payment agreements; the determination by the IRS that the balance due is not currently collectible; an offer-in-compromise (partial payment); and taxpayer bankruptcy.

Each product's cost is the sum of the resources devoted to the activities that form the product process. For example, Alternative Action breaks down into three activities: work up a tax case, resolve the case, and monitor the results of the case. Each of these activities has its own boundaries.

Below the activity level are tasks, and underneath them are steps. Usually, this level of detail is not shown in the business and cost models developed by activity costing and management. Instead, they appear in flowcharts and procedures manuals used by line supervisors and employees. We advise you to avoid gathering information on tasks and steps when you initiate activity costing and management—it could take years. Instead, allow people who work in activities to do this as they develop improvements of their operations.

As just discussed, classifying an organization's work according to activities and activity level has several advantages. First, it gives your organization a common language with which to discuss operations and their improvement. Second, it helps identify redundant or duplicative work (i.e., having four different security clearance activities in the same organization). Finally, looking at an organization as a dynamic hierarchy of activities gives you a perspective on the relationship of activities that often is masked by static organizational charts.

Let's look at two more key terms—resources and cost objects—before discussing how to gather activity information.

Resources

Organizations draw upon varying, but finite, quantities of resources to accomplish specific goals. Resources include the quantities of people, technology, materials, office space, and other elements generally required to meet those goals.

Another way of saying resources is "money"—from taxpayers, license fees, sales of goods and services, leases, fines, and all other sources of government revenue. ABC describes resources in monetary terms because everyone understands what a dollar means. ABC will sometimes describe resources as labor hours or full-time-equivalents, but these are only substitutes for dollar amounts.

Cost objects

Activities exist to make, deliver, and support an organization's products and services, which are known in ABC as *cost objects*. Cost objects include credit union loans, geophysical maps, or diagnostic tests—the major, and sometimes final, outputs of processes. For some ABC analyses and reports, cost objects can be individual customers or customer groups, specific projects, or contracts with outside organizations. In Chapter 5, you will see why cost objects are useful concepts.

Collecting Activity Information

Now that you understand ABC's basic terminology and concepts, you are ready to collect information to build an activity dictionary and different types of models of your operations. This information may be developed in a variety of ways. Some organizations assign specialists to observe the activities of departments or processes under review, or interview managers about them. They submit a draft dictionary to managers for comments and revisions. Others use an existing work breakdown structure as a starting point, modifying it as needed to reflect a process perspective instead of the usual project or function orientation of these systems.

These are good methods, but they have some limitations. Observation can be time-consuming and often does not show the whole picture of work, especially over extended periods. Our experience is that the farther away managers work from line operations, the less they know about specific activities. Finally, most government operations do not have detailed work breakdown structures. As a rule, all you will find are job descriptions or outdated, misleading procedure manuals.

We believe that storyboarding is one of the best methods for government operations that have little or no activity information. It is also a way to involve supervisors and key employees in developing activity information. This helps ensure buy-in and support for what may become a new way of management. Observation can be used to validate the results of storyboarding, however.

Activity storyboarding

"Storyboard" is a term first used by the film industry, where scene-by-scene actions of a movie script are sketched like comic strips and pasted on a piece of cardboard. In ABC the "story" shows a rough sequence of distinct activities that make up a process.

The first step in activity storyboarding is to "brainstorm" and agree on all the activities that make up a process. Then participants sequence the activities to show how work flows through a process. Next they define the activities, usually with a few sentences about their purpose and tasks. Finally, they identify the outputs of each activity and process and the customers for these outputs. The results of this exercise are used to produce activity dictionaries, charts of activities, or models of processes.

Here's an example of storyboarding as it was used by a government contractor. The same approach has been used by several other civilian and defense organizations.

Storyboarding at EG&G Mound Applied Technologies

If you've ever visited NASA's Mission Control room in Houston, you'll remember that there's not much to say about it. It's smaller than it looks on TV and is distinguished only by the number of bright computer screens lined up from one end of the room to the other.

What's important in that room—to the astronauts and observers alike—is what's happening on-screen at each workstation. The decisions made at those workstations can make or break a mission and save or lose lives.

You'd have the same sort of feeling participating in one of several activity management storyboarding sessions at EG&G Mound Applied Technologies, a U.S. Department of Energy (DOE) management and operations contractor. Because EG&G used electronic meeting software, or "groupware," for these sessions, the room looks a bit like Mission Control. There are a dozen bright blue computer screens illuminating the windowless room, and a large screen in front. As in Houston, managers and employees busily enter information on computers. On the surface, it's a familiar scene, and even a bit mundane.

But a lot is riding on what these people do in this dimly lit room. There's EG&G Mound's survival, for one thing. Unless it can reduce costs quickly, the company could lose its contract with DOE. Across-the-board layoffs won't do: the people at Mound handle nuclear material, and willy-nilly budget cuts might throw out the baby with the bathwater. EG&G managers have to make some tough decisions about how the company can improve its operations to run them with far fewer employees. For another, there's the successful conversion of Mound's nuclear weapons facilities to productive peacetime public and private business.

That's why Mound is starting at ground zero, building a new model of its operations using activities and processes instead of old-fashioned functional boxes on an organization chart.

Is it a task, activity, or process? Anyone who has made a career in government has gone through the debate of the difference between a goal and an objective at least a dozen times. Likewise, at first no one agrees 100 percent on the difference between a task and an activity, or an activity and a process (most people agree on steps, though). But that's okay, because no hard and fast lines divide the three levels of work. In fact, debating the demarcations is the first step (or is it activity?) toward taking a process perspective of your organization.

For example, early during a storyboarding session at EG&G Mound, a typical question posed over the rattling of computer keys was "Is doing your time card an activity?" With a facilitator's help, participants came to understand that the act of doing one's time card was a task, but that "time-keeping" in general might be viewed as an administrative activity.

As the session progressed, more and more activities appeared on each participant's screen and, eventually, on the large screen at the front of the room. At this point, discussions arose over how items like "committee meetings" should be defined. "Is attending meetings an activity, part of an activity, or a process in itself?" wondered several participants. Again, with guidance, the group concluded that a committee meeting wasn't a process in itself, but a task in an activity that is part of a process that generates a product.

The group gradually developed a list of processes and a group of activities associated with each process from the raw data they had entered into the system a short time before. By the end of the three-hour session, everyone had spoken at least once and the group members had a rough draft of processes and activities to call their own.

Equally important, members of the group had started to have a process perspective toward their work. When they did, it was hard not to reach this conclusion: *permanently reducing costs without sacrificing customer satisfaction must come from improving business processes.*

Manual methods of storyboarding. You need not use computerized groupware for storyboarding. Many organizations have group members write processes and activities on note cards, then arrange them in the correct order by taping them to a wall. The result is the same as using groupware, but is much slower and more cumbersome. Any large, complex organization should consider using groupware instead.

Creating Data Bases of Activity Information

Once you have gathered activity data, how do you store and retrieve it? In a small organization that does a few simple operations, it is easy to do this manually or with a simple computer program such as a spreadsheet. More complex organizations need a computerized relational data base to do this, one that uses unique numeric codes for each activity.

A data base is a logically organized collection of related information. For example, an activity dictionary is a data base of activity definitions. A relational data base allows you to link information stored in different data bases or tables. This "link-up" capability lets you look at activity information from several perspectives, each of which affords new insight into how you do business. We will discuss this capability further on in this section.

You can buy inexpensive (and also expensive) off-the-shelf activity-based costing software to create a relational data base on a personal computer or minicomputer. You also can build it from scratch with commercial data base software, such as d-Base, R-Base, and Paradox. Choose carefully, and be prepared to make trade-offs between ease of use and degree of sophistication.

Creating Different Views of Activities

Different issues and challenges require you to approach an organization in different ways. For example, a safety manager could aggregate all activities related to an organization's safety into an activity center for looking at total safety costs. An *activity center* is simply a report on a set of linked or related activities. In the shipyard example in Chapter 1, the costs of all job order planning activities, no matter where they reside in an organizational chart, can be aggregated into a single activity center called "job order planning."

On the other hand, an organizational model would show the processes and activities that reside within each department or function in an agency. The noncost information in the right-hand column of Figure 1-6 is an example of the view of operations offered by an organizational model. As you can see by the figure, you can accumulate activity costs in this model that, in total, correspond to a line-item budget.

Let's say you want to look at activity information arranged by cross-functional processes. You would review the organizational model and activity dictionary and assign each process to a cross-functional process. If you are using a relational data base, a command to the computer would cause it to link the processes together in a special report, regardless of where the processes are done in your organization. This process model view of your organization is useful for process management, improvement, and planning new information systems.

By assigning relevant cross-functional processes to core business processes, you gain a *business model* view of how you make and deliver products and services to customers. This helps you understand "survive-or-die" operations. By assigning costs and cost objects to activities, you can create *cost models* and *bills of activities*. These help you understand the true costs of processes, and what causes those costs. We will discuss them more in Chapter 5.

Bill of activities: A list of the activities consumed by a cost object, along with their costs and other information.

Activity Attributes

While analyzing activities, you may want to look at their different attributes. An attribute is a specific characteristic that may vary among different activities.* For example, an activity can have one or more of these attributes:

---

* Not to be confused with attributable costing.

- **Value attribute**: An activity may be value added (it increases the value of a product or service) or non-value added (it adds cost, but not value, to the product). Chapter 6 discusses value analysis in detail.

- **Cost-of-quality attribute**: Some activities will fall into one of the four cost-of-quality variables—prevention, appraisal, internal failure, or external failure. Chapter 3 shows the benefit of using this type of analysis for targeting process improvements.

- **Activity level**: An activity level describes which part of an operation an activity supports and indicates its nature. This classification is important for costing, as you will see in the next chapter. For example:

  — *Unit* activities are done for every unit of output produced by a process. Putting letters into envelopes is a unit activity done on every letter mailed.

  — *Batch* activities are done on a group of outputs. Carrying boxes of letters to a mail box is a batch activity.

  — *Customer* activities are done to support individual or groups of customers. This would include communicating with a customer, answering complaints, or arranging certain services.

  — *Organization* activities are done to support an entire organization. Preparing strategic plans is an organization activity.

Activity levels can include product or service, facility, process, department, function, or other categories, depending on what you find useful.

There are many other types of activity attributes—as many as you want and need. Each opens up a new avenue of studying how your organization operates. The foundation for them is a good activity dictionary that describes each activity with enough detail to allow for accurate classification.

Consensus Is Important

Any one or all of these activity development methods may meet your organization's needs. Whichever you use, remember that achieving consensus on definitions is vital to the success of any activity costing or management effort. Always have managers sign off on their unit's activities and activity dictionary definitions. Review the results with everyone so that they understand the system.

Summary

Organizations are hierarchies of activities that range from the smallest task to enterprise processes. Improvement happens when you change some part of an activity, such as its inputs, transformation components, or outputs.

The building blocks of activity costing and management are an activity dictionary and information as to where activities reside. With a relational data base, you can use this information to develop several models that offer different perspectives on an organization. Even without cost figures, activity information shows the relationships of activities to each other, to outputs, and to customers.

New Principles from Chapter 4

Activity Basics

Because this chapter was rather technical, we'll give you two easy warm-up examples—but you have to complete them.

Old Rule or Practice	New Principle or Practice
Improve process performance by telling people to work harder, or adding more money to a process.	
	Look at a process from several perspectives before deciding how to improve it.

Old Rule or Practice	New Principle or Practice

Chapter

5

Developing Cost Information

- ABC's strongest power is helping you understand the costs of activities and the relationship of those costs to products, services, projects, and customers. By understanding this "cause-and-effect" relationship, you are better able to control and improve processes.

- Conventional cost accounting systems distort an organization's understanding of its costs by hiding them in overhead or indirect accounts. Activity costing strives to trace these costs to the activities that use them.

- ABC's cost-finding process searches for factors responsible for the amount of resources consumed by activities. Called cost drivers and activity drivers, they also are used to allocate resources that cannot be traced directly to an activity.

- ABC cost finding is less a mechanical procedure and more an exploration of fundamental assumptions about how and why work is done. Thus, the act of creating ABC information is more important than the information itself.

"Without a financial model, many efforts may get directed to areas where there is not a lot of spending and where the gains from improvement are not that high. So developing an activity-based cost model first helps managers to set priorities. It lets them see where most of the dollars are being spent, what the fundamental drivers of those processes are, and where, if you can make changes, they can get big payoffs."

—Robert S. Kaplan, Harvard Business School and pioneer of Activity-Based Management

In the previous chapter, you learned to build an activity dictionary. In this chapter, we will discuss how to assign costs to the activities and processes listed in the dictionary. Also, you'll learn how to build a financial or cost model such as Dr. Kaplan discusses.

Key Terms and Concepts

What does ABC mean by "cost?"

Cost simply refers to the resources consumed by activities that make products and services. Usually you express resources in terms of dollars, but to managers it is often more important to state costs in terms of the resources being consumed, such as labor hours, gallons of gasoline, and so on. Whether called dollars, hours, or gallons, resources are finite, can be divided into measurable units, and have an identifiable market value.

All costs are controllable at some level of an organization; ultimately, legislators control the total cost of government. In ABC, however, "controllable cost" refers to those costs that an activity or process manager can control in a given period. One objective of ABC is to maximize this control.

Finally, all costs are caused by something. Finding and understanding that cause is the essence of activity-based costing.

Costing periods. Throughout this chapter we refer to "short-term costs," which are usually those that occur during one year or less. We recognize, however, that many government projects require many years, even decades, to produce their final output. Costing periods should be long enough to take into account peak or cyclical demand.

How much of your organization should be included in costing? In the best of all possible worlds, your initial effort will include all activities in your organization. This eliminates or minimizes distortions to the cost picture that result from having to allocate some costs the old overhead rate way. If you cannot include all of them, then at least cost out those that are most directly related to the main activities or the activities that interest you most.

Cost objects. Cost objects are the reasons why activities exist, which are as follows:

- To produce products and services customers want

- To sustain the organization that produces these products and services.

Cost objects can be major work-in-process outputs in a chain of linked activities, or the chain's final output that is delivered to external customers. A cost object also can be a customer or group of customers, including the entire "market" or constituency of a public organization. As shown in Figure 5-1, cost objects consume activities, which is why ABC first calculates the cost of the activities that go into making a cost object, then arrives at the cost of services and products.

Figure 5-1
Two Central
Concepts of ABC

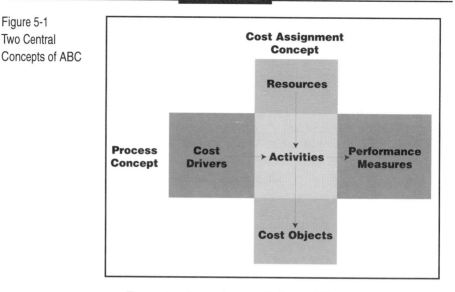

The *cost assignment concept* is that activities consume resources and cost objects consume activities

The *process concept* is that cost drivers affect resource consumption which in turn affects activity performance measures.

Activity driver. An activity driver is a measure of the frequency and intensity with which an activity is used to produce its output. For example, the number of inquiries received by an information center is an activity driver.

Cost driver. This factor is the root cause of changes in the amount of resources an activity consumes. The source of an inquiry (i.e., from citizens, the media, or Congress) may determine the amount of time spent responding to it, so the source is a cost driver.

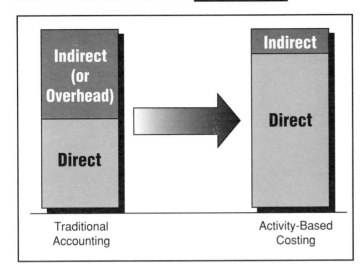

Figure 5-2
Indirect/Overhead
Expenses in
Traditional
Accounting and
Activity-Based
Costing

Sources of ABC Cost Information

ABC's cost-finding objective is to identify and trace all costs incurred in making a specific product or service to the activities that produce that output. In theory, this would mean there would be only so-called direct costs. But let's be realistic: unless your entire organization produces only one product or service, there will always be some costs that are not economical or practical to trace to a specific output so there will be some indirect or overhead costs in your calculations, which we will call nontraceable costs. Ideally, these will not exceed 10 percent of the total costs of a specific activity or output. Don't use this 10 percent figure as a benchmark, however; think about "materiality," an accounting term for "importance." A cost item is material if understanding it would influence decisions by internal or external customers, suppliers, and other stakeholders. In ABC material costs should be traced to specific activities to the extent feasible.

Importance is in the eye of the beholder. That one percent of an output's cost that goes for general support of a computer services department may not be material to a legislative committee, but knowing (and controlling) this cost might mean survival to computer department managers who compete with outside sources to produce the output. To find out what is material in your costs, ask the potential users of the information what they think is important.

With due consideration to materiality, here is general guidance on traceable costs under ABC. Traceable costs can be identified with and traced to a specific activity and then to an output:

- Labor: The salaries and other benefits for employees who work directly or indirectly on a specific output. Other benefits include health and life insurance, pensions, severance payments, training and counseling, continued health care, and unemployment and worker's compensation.

- Costs of recruiting, paying, evaluating, and other personnel functions related to a specific activity.

- Material and supplies consumed by an activity, including costs of ordering and handling them. Things like minor office supplies may not be worth tracing.

- Costs of inputs (i.e., products and services) received from other government entities or outside contractors, and used to produce a specific output.* This is the total cost of the input, starting with procurement planning and ending with contract close-out.

---

* Often, the "prices" charged for products and services provided by one government unit to another are subsidized. When these products are used to produce a receiving unit's outputs, such subsidies will understate the full cost of the outputs. For true full costing, the cost of an output received from another unit of the same government is that unit's full cost of producing it.

- Costs of office space, equipment, facilities, and utilities used by an activity to produce a specific output.

In theory (again), all ABC cost information can be traced from an organization's general ledger accounts to activities and then to outputs, but this is usually true only if you produce one product or service.

In reality, if your organization is moderately complex, you will need to do a special study of activity costs. You conduct this study at the start of your ABC initiative, and periodically repeat all or parts of it to capture changes in operations. How often you repeat the study will depend on the frequency of changes to your processes and activities.

Because labor is usually far and away the major expense in the line items of government operations budgets, it makes sense to first focus on personnel costs.

Labor costs

Besides costing, another reason for focusing on personnel first is to understand how your people spend their time. What people do and how they do it are the most powerful determinants of efficiency and productivity. You found part of the answer when you set up processes and activities. Now find out which activities count the most toward resource consumption.

Below are four key steps in determining labor costs:

1. Get a list of the people in the organization units for which you developed activity lists.

2. Find out the salary of each person on the list, along with job category, classification, or job description. Later on, knowing the job information lets you analyze whether someone's work is appropriate to his or her job classification.

3. Determine the percent of time that individuals spend doing specific activities over a designated period (usually, one year). If you sum the percentages, you will have the number of full-time equivalents (FTEs) engaged in an activity. For example, 10 people who spend 10 percent of their time on an activity equal one FTE, as do two people who spend half their time on an activity.

Remember from the IRS example in Chapter 2 that FTEs can be a misleading item of information, however, because high-salaried employees are counted the same as those with lower salaries. That's another reason for coding people's job classifications and salaries.

4. Multiply time percentages by annual salaries, add in a benefits multiplier, and sum the results by activity. This gives you total direct labor costs.

Step 3 is the most difficult. Your alternatives (and you may choose to use a couple of them) are:

- **Time cards and reports.** If you have a sophisticated, process-oriented work breakdown structure (WBS), often you can derive much of the information you need from it. This is especially true if the WBS codes include job number and task indicators. If you do not have a WBS, you can eventually use ABC to help develop one that suits your needs.

- **Interviews with managers.** This involves asking managers how much time they think their people spend doing the various activities in a process. However, experience shows that managers do not always know how much time their employees devote to the many extra things that have been tasked to them over the years. These include other departments' reporting requirements, special assignments that never went away, and myriad other items unrelated to a primary mission.

- **Observation**. In functions such as building maintenance and repetitive industrial operations, you often can, with stopwatch in hand, observe and record how much time people spend on certain tasks and activities. As noted in Chapter 4, this method has limitations, but it is a useful way to validate interviews with managers and surveys.

- **Surveys.** Here, you simply ask people who work in an operation how much time they spend doing specific activities. The larger your organization and the more removed managers are from actual operations, the more a survey approach makes sense.

For their first foray into activity costing, we think most government organizations should rely on the survey approach: people who do the work usually have the best picture of how they spend their time. Like storyboarding, surveys are one more way to involve people in activity costing and management, and if people contribute to developing costs, they are more likely to believe them.

Surveying for labor cost information

Your first decision is whether to survey all or a sample of the employees about a set of activities. In smaller activities, it is best to survey everyone. In large, homogenous activities a sample will save you time and money. A word of caution: if you have many groups or field sites that do the same activity, be sure to include a representative sample of each in the survey so that you can do some intergroup comparisons. This is because different work units and field sites tend to evolve their own rules and procedures over time.

Figure 5-3
Survey
Questionnaire

Employee Name	Organization Code
Jane Smith	150

Business Function: PROVIDE ADMINISTRATIVE SUPPORT

Process #	Process Name	Percent of Time:
12001	Analyze and Prepare Reports	_____
12002	Control Documents	_____
12003	Provide Personnel Services	_____
12004	Manage Distribution/Pick-up and Delivery	_____
12005	Perform Paperwork Management	_____
12006	Perform Equipment Services	_____
12007	Provide Specialty Services	_____
12008	Perform Administrative/Clerical Duties	_____
12009	Training	_____

Employee Total: _____

All process percentages must add up to 100%

Employee Signature _____

Your survey instrument is simply the list of activities developed for a particular work unit. As shown in Figure 5-3, you may want to add some "Other" categories to capture those stray tasks and assignments missed earlier.

When you survey individuals, it is important to validate the results with their managers. What happens if the way in which an employee allocates time differs greatly from what a manager expects? Meet with the employee to ensure that he or she understands the meaning of the activity list and the survey process. If there was no procedural error, chances are the employee is right. Helping the manager understand the discrepancy underscores the power of ABC and can gain you his or her support during the early stages of introducing this new approach. (Be extremely diplomatic about this, though: egos are involved. Meet with each manager individually, in private, to go over the results of his or her unit.)

Summarizing labor cost and FTE information is simple—if you have a relational data base or ABC software package such as that described in Chapter 4. The work will be much more complicated and time-consuming if you have to use computer spreadsheets or manual calculators. Either way, you are simply summing the labor resources devoted to each activity, in both FTEs and dollars, to produce cost model tables such as those shown in Figure 5-4.

Process/Activity	Dollars	FTEs*
Perform Personnel Duties		
Interview personnel	$20,261	0.48
Hire/discipline/fire personnel	5,782	0.14
Monitor EEO program	8,394	0.20
Perform appraisals	12,486	0.30
Perform time-keeping duties	7,753	0.24
Develop, revise position descriptions	10,130	0.24
Counsel employees	20,500	0.49
Schedule leave	11,480	0.27
Prepare paper or suggestions	9,686	0.23
Total	$106,472	2.53
*FTE = Full-time equivalent		

Figure 5-4 Cost Model for "Perform Personnel Duties" Process

Expenses other than labor

Tracing these costs can be easy or difficult, depending on the degree of sophistication of existing cost accounting information. Much depends on your purpose for using ABC. Under a full cost recovery policy or when you compete with outsiders to provide a service, you want to record all expenses with great precision, but if your initial purpose is process improvement or restructuring operations, and nonlabor costs are a small part of your budget, less detail is required. (This is, of course, for the time being. Later on, you will want to refine your cost capture system to account for all expenses.)

The first step is to *understand your general ledger accounts* and how they accumulate costs: how cost collection is done and what data are available in what level of detail. In most government organizations, this information is available in several formats and accounts—none of which are attributed to activities. Your accounting professionals' assistance will be valuable in gaining this understanding.

Second, *directly assign expenses when possible.* Normally, expenses such as travel, materials, supplies, and outside contracts are the easiest to trace and assign directly to a specific activity. For example, the cost of a contract for disposing of hazardous waste would be directly assigned to the activity "identify and dispose of hazardous waste." If a facility or item of equipment is dedicated to a single activity, then all its costs are traced to that activity. In every case, however, be sure that you and activity managers understand and agree on an expense assignment.

Beware of hidden or inaccurate costs when you make these direct assignments. For example, the cost of a contract is not only the amount paid to the vendor, but also the cost of contract procurement and administration. Some organizations track this cost by contract number, which means you can trace it. Others simply add a percentage of all procurement and administration costs to every contract amount, or lump it into an overhead account allocated by some other means. Although allocation is an economical and practical method, it should reflect all costs accurately. The next step helps ensure this.

Third, *use cost drivers and activity drivers to allocate costs you cannot trace.* Traditional cost accounting uses arbitrary formulas such as allocating an equal portion of overhead or indirect expenses to labor hours. In Chapter 2, we called this "peanut butter accounting." We said that it distorts the cost picture because most activities in moderately complex organizations do not consume the same amount of so-called overhead or indirect expense.

Cost Drivers and Activity Drivers

The cost of output, or the cost object of an activity, is a function of one or more cost drivers and one or more activity drivers. This is true for both traceable and nontraceable costs. For example, if, in a year, an activity requires 50 (activity driver) simple (cost driver) purchase orders that average $30 each to prepare, then it consumes $1,500 in purchase orders. If the activity produces 100 units of output per year, then the average cost of purchase orders per unit is $15. Let's examine this calculation more closely.

As shown in Figure 5-1, a cost driver is a factor that is the root cause of changes in the amount of resources an activity consumed. For example, proofreading a draft document for spelling errors can be a manual procedure that takes several hours. If the document is on a computer disk, it can be checked in a few minutes with word processing software. Here, the cost driver is the format of the document: paper or computer disk.

Many activities have several cost drivers, as shown in these examples:

Activity:	Evaluating bids
Cost Driver:	Number of bidders
	Number of reviewers
Activity:	Negotiating contracts
Cost Driver:	Multiple or sole-source contracts
	Fixed-price or price-plus-fixed-fee contract
Activity:	Preparing purchase orders
Cost Driver:	Complexity of order (perhaps measured by line items per pur–chase order)
	Amount of Purchase Order
	Contract vehicle

Activity:	Transporting equipment to field sites
Cost Driver:	Type of vehicle used
	Time of day or week

Activity:	Providing heating, ventilation, and air conditioning (HVAC)
Cost Driver:	Square feet of facility used by an activity
	Type of environment required (office, shop, computer room)

Through cost drivers you can understand why and how the level of resources for any task varies and adjust your allocations accordingly. For example, an activity may consume 100 purchase orders in a period, all of which are simple, low-cost buys. Another also consumes 100 orders, but these are complex, high-cost purchases. Instead of charging the same purchase order cost to each activity, it is more accurate to use a lower cost factor for simple purchase orders, and a higher cost factor to those that are more complex.

While cost drivers affect how an activity consumes resources, activity drivers affect demand for those resources. In the example of the draft document, the number of drafts (the activity driver) determines how many times proofreading will be done. The number of errors in a draft (also an activity driver) determines how much time will be spent correcting them, so it is a measure of level of intensity. Other examples include the following:

Activity:	Evaluating bids
Activity driver:	Number of contracts or purchases

Activity:	Transporting equipment to field sites
Activity Driver:	Number of transports
	Distance to field site

Activity:	Providing HVAC
Activity Driver:	Hours a day a facility is used
	Season of the year

Activity:	Accepting fee payments
Activity Driver:	Number of payments received

Activity:	Reconciling bank accounts
Activity Driver:	Number of bank accounts
	Frequency of reconciliation

Activity:	Maintaining vehicles
Activity Driver:	Number of vehicles
	Miles driven per vehicle
	Type of repairs needed

Note that there can be more than one activity driver for each activity, which together reflect both the frequency (volume) and intensity (amount per use) with which it is applied to a cost object.

Finally, let's apply *activity levels* to the activity drivers. As you recall from Chapter 4, an activity's level also indicates its nature. A unit activity is applied to each unit of output produced, and a batch activity is applied to a group of outputs. Let's say your organization wants to hire some rocket scientists. Advertising for them in professional journals is a batch cost: it is done to recruit several scientists, so the cost is divided among those you hire. Helping your new scientists fill out their employment forms is a unit cost, because it is done for each scientist individually. Also, look at Figure 5-5: this is a unit-level activity, done for every fee paid. "Daily close-out and review of clerks" is a batch activity, done for all payments received in a day.

Understanding an activity's cost and activity drivers is not as hard as you might think. Once they understand the basic concepts, people quickly identify and agree on cost drivers. There is usually some record of the demand for, or consumption of, the outputs of other activities, which allows activity drivers to be identified.

Having developed cost and activity drivers, you use them to allocate costs that cannot be directly traced to an activity. Usually this is done by calculating the total resources consumed by an activity that produces outputs used by other activities, then dividing it by the total volume of output in a year, adjusting for cost drivers. For example:

- The activity "recruit professional staff" produces 200 (activity driver) new hires (cost objects) per year, for a total recruiting cost of $875,000.

- Recruiting rocket scientists requires twice as much effort as that required for other professionals, so profession is a cost driver. This means that the 50 scientists hired averaged $7,000 to recruit, while other professionals cost $3,500 each.

- The activity "review rocket plans" hired three rocket scientists and two other professionals for a new project (cost object). This activity consumed $28,000 in recruiting costs: $21,000 for the scientists and $7,000 for the others.

Without cost drivers, the "review rocket plans" activity might have been assigned the average cost of recruiting all professionals ($875,000/200), multiplied by the five hired for it. This would be about $22,000, which is 22 percent less than the more realistic $28,000 figure.

By repeating this process throughout the activities of an organization, you arrive at just about the total resources consumed by the activities. Now let's get the rest of them.

To do this, allocate residual expenses through a reasonable formula. No matter how hard you try, there always will be a small amount of expense that must be allocated in the old-fashioned overhead rate way. These are nontraceable costs shared among two or more activities or outputs, but are not economical or practical to trace to a specific one. They can be allocated to an activity through a reasonable estimate or formula that takes into account the cost drivers of the activities that produce them. Examples include:

- General administration, basic research, some technical support, and security not otherwise easily traced to specific activities.

- Employee health, recreation, and cafeteria facilities for a multi-activity site.

- General operations and maintenance costs for buildings, equipment, and facilities that cannot be traced to specific activities.

Deciding which cost item goes into which category requires judgment. Also, changes in production methods and technology may alter the mix over time.

What is not included in activity costs?

When you add up all the costs associated with the types of activities just listed, there will be some activities and expenses left over. These may include the costs of:

- Restructuring your entire organization, including post-employment costs such as severance pay or early retirement incentives, and moving activities to another site as part of a general consolidation

- Closing or abandoning a facility (including nonrecurring clean-up costs)

- Costs associated with unused capacity.

Many agencies assign these expenses to their activities and outputs anyway, as a form of overhead or indirect cost (sometimes this is called "full absorption costing"). Not so in ABC because this artificially inflates the cost of making the outputs. Instead, you treat these costs as separate expenses because over the short term, managing them has nothing to do with producing an anticipated amount of output.

Again, you need good judgment here because in some cases you can justify assigning these costs to activities and outputs. For example, what if the reason for consolidating activities is to improve their performance and reduce expense? Then the cost of so doing is an investment that can be amortized over several periods.

Having done this, you have traced or allocated all costs associated with activities. Now you can assign these costs to cost objects.

Assigning Costs With Bills of Activities

For products or services, final output is the cost object of a chain of linked activities that produce it and deliver it to a customer outside the process. The cost of that final cost object is the sum of all outputs that were used to make it.

Figure 5-5 shows how this works for a government organization that charges user fees for a public service. The process shown is called "receiving and processing fee payments" whose cost object is "completed fee payment transaction." In this cross-functional process, fees are collected by six clerks at three sites and deposited daily in each site's local bank account. Banks process the payments and also the bad checks. Finance and accounting offices handle the rest of the activities. We present the information in the form of a bill of activities.

Note that this bill of activities captures all costs associated with the process (facility and administrative costs are captured as a percentage of activities such as "accept fee payment"). The final cost of the cost object of this process (completed fee payment transactions) is shown in total ($205,100) and unit ($1.34 per fee received and processed).

Combined with those of other processes such as "setting fee schedules" and "enforcing fees," this bill helps present a full picture of the core business process of collecting fees.

Activity	Output	Annual Volume Measure/Quantity	Cost per Unit	Total Cost
Accept fee payment	Accepted fee	150,000	$ 1.00	$150,000
Processing of payments by bank	Processed payments	150,000	.05	7,500
Processing of returned checks	Bad checks processed	1,500	25.00	37,500
Daily close-out and review of clerks	Daily fees checked	1,320	3.00	7,920
Consolidate and deposit receipts	Deposited receipts	220	2.00	440
Review and transfer funds	Transferred funds	3	250.00	750
Maintenance charges for bank accounts	Bank account	3	80.00	240
Reconciling bank accounts	Balanced account	3	250.00	750
Total				**$205,100**
Cost per payment received and processed				**$1.34**

Figure 5-5 Bill of Activities of "Receiving and Processing Fee Payments" Process

Bills of activity come in many forms but generally have these characteristics:

- They show all activities in a process in sequence

- Each activity is separate and distinct, and is displayed with its specific cost object

- They show costs per activity along with activity driver information and total cost for the process.

When important, the total life cycle of a cost object should appear in its bill of activity. This may begin with design costs and end with disposal.

In the private sector, different groups of customers have long been recognized as cost objects that can consume varying amounts of activities. In the example in Figure 5-5, working with customers who pay with checks requires a unique activity called "processing of returned checks." Likewise, organizational customers, including other activities and government agencies, consume different activities at different rates. Analyzing the "how" and "how much" of this consumption can lead to policy and procedure decisions on what to charge for services and how to improve them.

Activity Centers

Many organizations divide all or part of their operations into functional cost centers: work units or departments that do related types of work. Examples include print shops, a job order planning office, or an emergency room. Although ABC can generate accurate cost information for these cost centers, it is often more revealing to look at the costs of activity centers. These centers do not necessarily physically reside in an office or shop; instead, they are simply reports on activities that may be spread across an entire organization. Thus, the cost of the process of "job order planning" can include the costs of the job order planning office and related costs in all activities in other departments related to job order planning. At a higher level of the activity pyramid, the process of "acquiring new work" can be an activity center and include in its costs those of the job order planning activity center.

Building a Cost Model

In ABC the term "cost model" or "financial model" is something of a misnomer. ABC cost models are more than simply a list of activities and processes such as those shown in Chapter 4, with costs added in. Instead, they are more akin to a general-purpose financial management information system built around activities and processes. As information systems, they are capable of showing:

- The activities that make up operations, how they are used, the kind and amount of resources they consume, and what they produce (i.e., cost objects)

- The relationship among activities, processes, and core business processes

- Actual unit costs of outputs produced

- The factors and events that influence resource consumption by activities (i.e., cost drivers and activity drivers)

- High-cost versus low-cost activities, which is important to managers who must set priorities about process improvement.

Figure 5-5 is a cost model for the "receiving and processing fee payments" process. Figure 9-1 shows a higher-level model of Navy shipyard operations and so provides less detail than the previous figure. If we were to follow it down the hierarchy, however, we would find an increasing amount of information, such as that shown in Figure 5-5.

Such models have far more value for management decisions than conventional agency or program budgets, which are as close as most government organizations come to portraying how resources are used. For the next several chapters, we will show their value.

Summary

In this chapter, you saw the mechanics of developing ABC cost information. At several points we noted opportunities to work with others to explore why and how resources are consumed. These included interviewing managers, surveying employees, and discussing with both the outcomes of cost-finding studies. Doing this serves two purposes besides collecting data.

First, you have the opportunity to educate people about ABC. When they participate in the process of developing ABC information, they learn its principles and methods and are better able to take over this process later.

Second, involving people helps to win their support for ABC, and also for the changes that it will generate. By helping build the financial foundation for ABC, they are more willing to take part in constructing its framework—the special studies, reports, and other actions that will follow.

New Principles from Chapter 5

Developing Cost Information

Old Rule or Practice	New Principle or Practice

Old Rule or Practice	New Principle or Practice

Chapter

6

Analysis of Activity Information

- ABC analysis offers a variety of tools and methods for understanding costs and processes, including what drives costs, the costs of serving different customer groups, and the value of doing specific activities.

- Benchmarking analysis allows you to set performance standards derived from the best practices of other organizations. It is also a way to adopt and adapt the best features of other organizations' processes to your own organization.

". . .and yet the true creator is necessity, which is the mother of our invention."

—Plato, *The Republic*

"First, you have to know what's necessary."

—Gustav Plato, Coopers & Lybrand

How do you reinvent government? Certainly, as Plato the philosopher said, you must be motivated by compelling need. But without careful analysis, many managers respond to necessity with blind, scatter-shot actions. In this chapter you'll see how activity costing and management open managers' eyes to what must be done so they can target specific problems for improvement. It is this type of clearly defined necessity that leads to true invention.

Over the years, users of activity costing and management developed or adapted dozens of analytic methods and reports that cover nearly every aspect of operations. Figure 1-7 in the first chapter lists some of these areas. In this chapter, we describe a few that are especially useful to public managers in improving and reinventing their operations.

Cost Driver Analysis

Look closely at some cost drivers and you'll find opportunities for process improvement. For example, if "number of errors" drives the cost for a rework activity, you automatically know that a previous activity is causing those errors. Prevent the errors and you need neither the rework activity nor an inspection activity to find the errors. If "type of contract vehicle" is a cost driver in the activity "preparing purchase orders," then you might want to shift more purchases to the least costly vehicles. To test your understanding of cost drivers, look back at Figure 5-5. Can you spot a major cost driver of this process? Hint: Look at the largest costs. What could you do minimize that cost driver's effect?

In their first pass at cost driver analysis, many managers quickly choose the most obvious causes and let things go at that. This is a mistake, because their choices may be merely the symptoms of underlying root causes. Keep asking "Why?" about a potential cost driver, and you will get to its root cause. For example, a cost driver of an activity that writes purchase orders may be the number that must expedited or rushed through the system with special handling.

1. Question: "Why do we expedite these purchase orders?"

   Answer: "Because the operations units that need purchases tell us to."

2. Q. "Why do they tell us to expedite?"

   A. "Because normally we take 90 days to make a purchase."

3. Q. "Why do we take 90 days to make a purchase?"

   A. "Because we have a large backlog of requisitions."

4. Q. "Why do we have a large backlog?"

   A. "Because many of the requisitions we receive are incomplete or full of errors, and we have to correct them."

5. Q. "Why are they incomplete or full of errors?"

   A. "Because the requisition forms are too complex and operations people do not know how to fill them out."

This series of questions produced several potential cost drivers: "average number of days to make a purchase," "backlog," "number of requisitions with errors," "complexity of forms," and "skill level of requisition writers." Some are easier to quantify than others, but all are more useful for cost management and process improvement than "number of expedited purchase orders."

An organization can have "cultural" cost drivers, too. For example, in some military depots that overhaul aircraft, workers take great pride in producing "perfect" results. It is a commendable practice that is taken to extremes. For example, a worker may spend an hour burnishing a scratch or blemish that in no way affects the performance of the aircraft. This "goldplating" drives up the cost of an overhaul. Another such cost driver is the number of management layers a simple proposed action must pass through before it is approved. In strict "command-and-control" cultures, this can add significant costs to an activity.

As you can see, cost driver analysis is not cut and dried. Often, it is more management art than management science, a challenge that requires discussion, introspection, and creative thinking.

Customer Cost Analysis

As any health department will tell you, it costs more to visit patients in isolated, rural areas than to treat urbanites who come to a central clinic. Some customers of weapons systems development groups make many engineering change orders, others few. Agencies that make grants know that some grantees require more attention, and others less.

These costs all relate to doing business with specific customers or customer groups. These costs are not due to making or delivering a basic product or service, but to differences in customer characteristics or behavior.

Why account for these differences? Two reasons: to adjust cost, fee, or price figures for different customers; and to find ways to reduce expense for high-cost customers.
By creating customer activity centers it is possible to trace and analyze all customer service costs. For example, a "customer administration" center would include all activities

related to working with customers other than providing a basic product or service. This center might include inquiries, complaints, agreement negotiations, and reports to customers. Another activity center, "customer change orders," would include all activities needed to enact these orders. Other centers might focus on special transportation or handling requirements by one customer or groups of customers.

This helps accumulate total costs at the centers. To see differences among customers, you must classify them into different groups and assign a code to each. If it makes sense, major customers might get their own codes.

If it is cost-effective, you may want to begin tracing costs to these customers as part of your routine accounting and financial reporting. Code numbers will facilitate this, but most of the time you will do this through special studies, using activity center data to understand the activities and cost involved.

Value Analysis

Value analysis is the process of categorizing activities by their value attributes. The objective is to learn where and how you can maximize the value added to products and services, and minimize unneeded work, errors, rework, and other problems that add cost but not value. First, we will give some background on value analysis and discuss its importance. Then you'll see more detailed information on conducting this powerful form of process analysis.

Origins of value analysis

Value analysis as conducted in activity management originates in an older industrial method that carries the same name. For decades industrial engineers in factories have classified as value added those tasks that change the physical properties of materials. Raw materials have value added to them by the processes that form them into finished products, but the engineers classify as non-value added such tasks as moving work-in-process from one point to another, storing products until they are needed, and inspecting for errors. This is because moving, storing, and inspecting an item does not change its physical form. If the item does not change because of such tasks, then no value is added to it. A good example of this is shown in Figure 3-5 in Chapter 3, which applies the older industrial value analysis to making and delivering pizzas.

Value analysis in activity management

Industrial value analysis is somewhat neutral about the worth of the outputs delivered by a process. For example, an industrial value analysis perspective of the process of writing a report might point out some non-value added activities and tasks such as proofreading for and correcting spelling errors. It would not necessarily question the value of writing the report in the first place.

Value analysis in activity management, on the other hand, would ask: "Would the customer for the product made by this process be willing to pay for that report?" If the answer is no, then it is very likely that writing the document would be called non-value added. Such a report would either be eliminated or, if this was not possible, drastically curtailed.

Value classifications

There are two basic classifications of value shown in Figure 6-1. The word "customer" here refers to any external recipients of the outputs of a process or activity. Value added activities should be targeted for continuous improvement or reengineering. Non-value added activities should be targeted for elimination if an organization can survive without them.

Value added

- Activities that are absolutely essential to making and delivering a product or service the customer needs

- Activities that change the fit, form, or function of the final output delivered to customers

- Any work that increases the net worth of the output (quality, value) as perceived by the customer

Non-value added

- Any activity or resource used beyond what is absolutely essential to delivering the product the customer needs

- Those activities that can be eliminated with no deterioration of performance of value added activities

- Any work that does not transform inputs into outputs, such as supervision, reviewing work products, inspection, and rework

- Any work task or activity that can be eliminated if a previous task or activity is done right the first time

Figure 6-1
Activity Value
Classification

"Non-value added" is not a judgment of the inherent worth of an activity or a reflection on the people who do it. Not all non-value added work can or should be eliminated. For example, inspecting a report for errors is something you may want to eliminate; inspecting components of the space shuttle is not. Likewise, training programs that increase basic skills are non-value added but still important to an organization's success.

Indeed, most definitions of non-value added would include TQM, BPR, and even ABC. In theory, an organization can survive without these management initiatives (though for how long is uncertain), and some customers may question their connection to products and services (other customers may require you to use these approaches). Any non-value added activity that produces benefits in excess of its costs, however, should be retained until that activity is no longer necessary.

Every organization has to determine its own value added and non-value added classifications. It is wise to be tough and to remember to ask, "Would the customer pay for this?"

Benefits of value analysis

Here are some benefits of value analysis as reported by different government organizations.

Reduced costs. Teams conducting value analysis at one government facility found that more than 50 percent of its support resources were being poured into non-value added activities. It didn't take long to take advantage of these new insights. As one facility executive put it, "The magnitude of these activities showed us that we could easily expect to get at least a 20 to 25 percent reduction in support costs." Improvements included simply eliminating activities or reducing the resources devoted to them.

Reduced cycle time. At a government facility's purchasing office, buyers found out that the time-honored practice of getting serial approvals for buys wasted time without adding value to the purchase process. Analyzing process work flows revealed that several people were needed to approve a buy and that problem transactions often "ping-ponged" between units. This added no value to the item being bought or the product for which it was intended. The buyers sped up the buying process by revising it to include parallel instead of serial reviews.

Cleaning closets. Within every organization there are rules, procedures, and activities you think have to be done, but that are really self-created extra work or legacies of another era. For example, there are always so-called mandated non-value added activities. These include complying with the endless rules, regulations, and procedures demanded by lawmakers and regulatory organizations. Until you can get some relief from these you have to do them, even if customers are not even remotely interested in paying the bill.

Our experience is that you should be vigilant about these mandates. "Validating them is critical," said one shipyard manager. "In many cases, what we always thought were external Navy or Defense Department requirements were actually self-imposed. We could eliminate these requirements without higher-level approval."

Consensus. Without value analysis, people with different and largely subjective perspectives on what happens in a process can become mired in mutual misunderstandings that typically generate more heat than light on "how the whole mess got started." In fact, problems are often made worse because process participants have no way to discern which activities are essential to making a process work. By determining which activities are valuable from the customer's viewpoint, value analysis allows employees and customers to use a common frame of reference to refine processes and solve problems.

"Non-value added" can be an ugly term

Before concluding this discussion, we'd like to answer a question that's probably been on your mind for a few pages or so: "How do I deal with employees who discover that the activities they perform so assiduously are 'not valuable'?"

Some organizations decide to avoid potential misunderstandings by eliminating the terms "value added" and "non-value added" from their vocabularies. That's seldom necessary and possibly counterproductive. If you are committed to process improvement, you want to have a work force that understands how much customers value their efforts. One Coopers & Lybrand consultant who has facilitated many value analysis teams sums up this perspective nicely: "No one likes to think that what he or she is doing does not add value, and people are uncomfortable classifying someone else's job that way. So putting yourself firmly in the customer's shoes is essential for this type of analysis. That's the only way you can be objective."

How about those unsung-hero-like activities, the ones you have to perform regardless of what the customer thinks of them? It is important to know that there's a real difference between non-value added work and work that is simply useless. You can take pride in work that helps sustain an organization, even if it is not highly valued by customers. You can also have deep inner satisfaction for helping an organization and the nation move forward in its social or economic agenda. You can even be valued by top management for keeping headquarters' and lawmakers' heat away from the organization.

The object is not to let people become proud of doing useless work. Focus their attention on reducing the amount of resources needed for their non-value added processes. Reward them for improvements in cost and time savings and transfer the best workers to value added activities when openings become available.

Benchmarking

Benchmarking, write C.J. McNair and Kathleen Leibfried in *Benchmarking: A Tool for Continuous Improvement*, seeks to "understand existing processes or activities, and then to identify an external point of reference, or standard, by which that activity can be measured or judged." Many organizations use benchmarking to compare the performance of one of their processes to that of outside processes. The wisest organizations use benchmarking in a more powerful way: to find processes that face the same challenges as

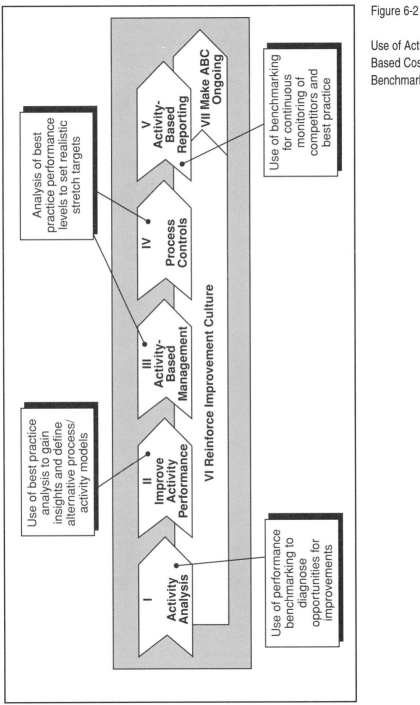

Figure 6-2

Use of Activity-Based Costing in Benchmarking

an internal process, no matter what they produce or in what type of industry they operate. ABC is essential in both cases.

Understanding the old process

Benchmarking begins by understanding the "as-is" process. With activity costing and management you can produce information on "as-is" levels of performance in terms of costs, cycle time, and other factors. You can also map the process with an activity map at first and then with more detailed flowcharting if necessary as shown in Figure 6-2. Now you have a baseline. Simply doing this will help you discover potential improvements.

Internal benchmarking

Comparisons can start internally, according to Leibfried, such as the documented ability of one field office to handle a procurement process in a distinctly more effective way than any of its counterparts. Internal benchmarking efforts that are based on activity information, and not on the out-of-context "numbers comparisons" that passed for best practices analysis in the past, may very well provide all the answers you need to improve or redesign a process.

In fact, she says, "It's wrong not to look internally. It gives you the ability to solve problems at a lower cost by finding the information you need down the hall. Also, it may cause you to set new priorities for the benchmarking effort because you learn more about your operations."

Some examples of internal benchmark performance comparisons include the following:

- Time required to do a type of report in one office, compared with that needed in another

- The cost of serving a particular type of customer or producing a product or service in one field site versus another

- The level of customer satisfaction with the services of one office compared with another.

Using activity costing helps validate the performance of the potential benchmark process. Activity mapping lets you record how it works.

Should you automatically adopt the procedures of the benchmark process? No, because good processes can become even better with vigorous improvement. You also may need to modify the benchmark process before installing it in other locations.

External benchmarking

If you discover that no internal process has the answers you need, then, according to Leibfried, "it's time to go outside and do external benchmarking to find the answer." This is where ABC can be extremely valuable because it allows you to avoid "apples to oranges" comparisons of your activities with those of other organizations. Erroneous comparisons are a major cause of benchmarking project failure.

In the private sector, companies frequently benchmark their performance against that of competitors. This lets them see where they stand in relation to an industry leader. There are problems with this, though. Usually only the more visible performance measures are available: price, product or service features, time-to-deliver, and customer satisfaction. Surveys asking consumers to compare one company's product or service with those of its competitors can yield customer information. No company is going to reveal the secrets of its most valuable processes to competitors, so finding out how they work is difficult if not impossible.

Government organizations tend not to have these problems, or at least have them to a lesser degree. One government almost always will help another in a benchmarking project. Most public organizations do not compete directly with private companies, so companies are more open to sharing their secrets. In fact, public-spirited companies like Xerox have policies and programs to share benchmark information with governments.

The standard of excellence you seek is an approach taken by a company or public agency that typifies the best way a process can be implemented. This can be a process that makes the same product as yours. By adopting, improving, and adapting it, you will equal, or even surpass, the organization you benchmarked.

Major breakthroughs in performance often come about by taking a different strategy. This is to search out a best practice that delivers the same results needed from your process, but that has somewhat different outputs. When you do this, usually you leapfrog past performance levels of all organizations that do pretty much what you do.

For example, Xerox faced lethal competition for the copy machine market from Canon and other competitors some years ago. One problem was response time to customer and field office orders for parts and supplies. To ensure a performance breakthrough, Xerox did not look for the best practices of the copier or other similar industries. Instead, it sought out any companies that were high performers in distributing small orders of a large variety of items and meeting customer requirements that bound them to respond to requests within 24 hours. Xerox found the answer to its prayers in catalog retailer L.L. Bean, which has one of the best records in the world of meeting such challenges.

"Xerox looked at L.L. Bean and sought to understand its distribution process operations, costs, and results," says Leibfried. "Then Xerox developed improvements to that process and adapted it to distributing copier parts and supplies. Today, the company is the copier industry leader in parts and supplies distribution."

As in internal benchmarking, activity costing and management help you understand an external best practice and how to adopt, adapt, and improve it. Even when you do not have all the facts about a best practice, activity management can help you "reverse engineer" parts of it to complete the picture.

Benchmarks as standards

Most public agencies look inward for performance standards. Doing a little better than the year before, or at least not doing worse, is acceptable for performance. When justifying a capital investment, most of the time it is enough to say, "It will help us become 10 percent better."

In activity management, the standard often is the best practice in a process or operation. Investments are judged on whether they will help surpass, or at least draw even with, this best practice. This gives an external focus to improvement that sparks a search for best practices.

Summary

In activity cost and management, analysis is a combination of data, questions, and introspection. The data are hard, accurate, and objective, as are the questions.

In cost driver analysis, questions help you get to the root cause of resource consumption, which often leads to process improvement. In customer analysis, you gain understanding of cost differences in serving different customers and groups that helps to determine fees and ways to cut costs.

In value analysis, you discover how to eliminate or reduce resources to activities that add cost but not value to products and services delivered to customers.

Benchmarking analysis gives you external standards for judging internal operations. More important, it allows you to profit from the success of processes in other organizations.

New Principles from Chapter 6

Analysis of Activity Information

Old Rule or Practice	New Principle or Practice

Old Rule or Practice	New Principle or Practice

Chapter

7

ABC Projects, Controls, and Information Systems

- Initial ABC projects often take the form of assessments focused on mapping, costing, and modeling business processes. Executing these efforts usually combines an organization's normal project management system with special steps that ensure the integrity and utility of ABC information.

- Many first-time ABC projects fail because they do not define the customers for their results, or they lose sight of their original objectives and scope.

- Risk management should be thought of as establishing performance and control objectives for a given activity or process and measurements of that performance. Activity compliance reports can be prepared to examine an organization's compliance framework or the effectiveness of compliance processes.

- ABC has only recently begun to be incorporated into mainstream financial and management information systems, but the availability of better systems technology has accelerated its adoption.

"Cheshire Puss," Alice began, rather timidly, "Would you tell me please, which way ought I to go from here?"

"That depends a good deal on where you want to get to," said the Cat.

"I don't much care where —" said Alice.

"Then it doesn't matter which way you go," said the Cat.

—Lewis Carroll, *Alice's Adventures in Wonderland*

If, like Alice, you are not clear about where you want new financial and management information to take you, then the Cheshire Cat is correct: how you implement ABC is irrelevant. Although most of this chapter focuses on how to conduct technical aspects of ABC projects, the most critical part of the next few pages concerns defining the objectives of those undertakings.

Most ABC and Activity-Based Management efforts start out with one or a few assessment projects, so we will first present an implementation framework for conducting an initial assessment. Next we describe how to use ABC to establish better cost management, internal controls, and risk management. Finally we provide an approach to conducting a requirement analysis for an ABC financial and management information system.

Conducting Initial ABC Projects

The initial technical phase of an ABC project usually assesses activities by collecting, analyzing, and reporting on their structure, relationships, costs, drivers, and other components. Most organizations have procedures for project planning and management that can be used for such assessments, so we will not propose a formal planning method here. We will talk instead about scoping the technical aspects of the assessment, communications and resource planning, personnel, training, presenting findings, and getting a commitment for action.

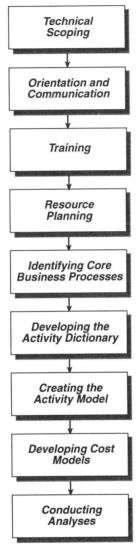

Figure 7-1
Steps in
Conducting an
ABC Assessment

Technical scoping

In Chapter 12 we discuss the need to understand the strategic intent of conducting an ABC assessment before going into its technical design. Here we will focus on different technical approaches to assessment.

- Some organizations use ABC solely to develop accurate cost data for products and services. When the U.S. Bureau of Engraving started competing with private companies for U.S. Postal Service business, it did activity cost estimating for stamp-making processes. This type of assessment involves few people, is relatively low-cost and quick, and focuses on one or a family of related services, products, and processes.

- Navy shipyards' purpose for ABC was to eliminate or reduce resources devoted to non-value added support work, reconfigure a reduced work force, and centralize some support functions. This is a complex undertaking, moderately costly, and involves nearly every part of the shipyard community. Gathering and analyzing the necessary data took only a few months at each shipyard, although each yard employs several thousand workers.

- The Internal Revenue Service is using Activity-Based Management as a key element in basic management philosophy and incorporating ABC into its plans to upgrade a complex financial and management information system. This approach takes longer, costs more, and involves everyone in the organization. It develops internal capability, however, which saves money and enhances results in the long term.

Once you understand the basic approach you will take, you need to specify the following:

- What type of information an ABC assessment is expected to deliver, when, to whom, and in what format

- How people will use that information to control and improve activities

- Performance parameters for the assessment, including data accuracy and usefulness and resulting improvements to activities

- The people, processes, and information systems that will be involved in the project or initiative, and those that will be targeted for change

- How ABC will tie into other improvement initiatives (see Chapters 3 and 12)

- Whether you will have pilot projects, and how you will use their results for further development throughout your organization (more on this in Chapter 12).

If you intend to introduce ABC as a permanent component of your financial and management information system, you would be wise to examine the human and organizational aspects of doing this before starting on an initial assessment. The results of this examination may affect the way you design the assessment. Chapter 11 discusses human and organizational issues at length. In Appendix B you will find a long list of questions to ask about introducing ABC to an organization.

Orientation and communication

Develop a briefing for managers of business units where you will be collecting information. To let them know the purpose of the project and gain the cooperation you will need from them deliver the briefing before you begin introducing ABC.

Develop a communications plan to let everyone in the organization know what you will be doing and why. This type of communication is discussed at length in Chapter 11.

Training

If you use the storyboard methods discussed in Chapter 4, you will need a one- or two-hour orientation and training course for storyboard session participants. Likewise, you will need a short course on reviewing activity mapping and costing results for managers whose activities are targeted for assessment. If you involve managers in cost-driver or other analysis, a short training module on this will be useful. It's best to deliver all this training immediately before people have to use their new skills and knowledge.

Resource planning

The resources needed for an assessment are in direct proportion to the number of business units or activities covered and the availability of existing data on them. To determine the former, look at your organization chart and decide which units to include in the analysis, based on the flow of the core business processes that interest you.

Unfortunately, there are no "economies of scale" in collecting the data. If you intend to look at all activities in a major business unit that is involved in several core business processes, then plan to conduct three or four storyboard sessions in it. If you investigate 10 such business units, plan on 10 overview briefings and 30 to 40 storyboard sessions.

You are ahead of the game if you have an existing work breakdown structure or coded time-keeping system because that sometimes can be tied into activity analysis. You also have an advantage if you are well advanced in applying quality management or looking at cross-functional processes because you will have already mapped your processes and activities. These are at least starting points and they will make it easier for people to understand and accept activity analysis and costing information.

Data entry and data base technicians are essential for large activity assessment projects. Data entry time is directly proportional to the number of time estimation forms (see Chapter 4) you collect from each employee. You will need relational data base software to construct and analyze activities and costs.

Core business processes

As discussed in Chapter 4, an organization has many cross-functional processes that transcend the boundaries of business units such as departments and divisions. A few of these are core business processes, the "survive-and-thrive" operations of the organization. An executive steering committee or a larger group of executives and senior managers should identify these core processes before you attempt to map them. This provides a framework for data collection, coding, and analysis.

Developing the core process list is the initial executive task in managing by activities instead of by functions. It requires executives to identify and define external customers and their expectations—often for the first time. Each executive must think "out-of-the-box" of his or her function, looking instead (almost always for the first time) at how work flows cross-functionally. The participants must reach consensus on the results because without support at the top there will be no action after the assessment.

Developing the activity dictionary

This step's objective is to build an activity dictionary that describes operations and an activity hierarchy that codes activities for analysis. It is one of the first steps needed to win support for activity methods among business unit managers.

Our approach is to collect activity data by business unit and then reconfigure it by cross-functional processes. We start the collection procedure by orienting key managers. Then we have each group of managers identify business processes conducted within their units using a modified storyboard format. The results are the foundation for later storyboarding sessions that identify the activities associated with each business process.

As with executives identifying core business processes, this gets managers thinking in terms of activities instead of outputs or lower-level tasks. It also gives them an experience similar to that of the activity storyboard sessions so they will better understand the results of those sessions.

Collecting activity data

Activity storyboarding sessions such as those discussed in Chapter 4 are best conducted with a dozen people from within a business unit who operate processes that produce one or a family of similar outputs. The group spends four to six hours brainstorming and sequencing a list of all activities conducted within their sphere of operations. Participants and their managers need to validate the results of these sessions, which helps ensure their agreement with later analyses of the information.

When you get the results of all storyboard sessions, you develop an organization-wide dictionary that defines each activity. Preparing a manageable document often requires creating some standard activities such as planning, coordinating, and so on. You need to have managers agree on these standard definitions.

Creating activity models

This involves arranging processes and their activities and linking them to your organization's business units. After this, as shown in Chapter 4, you assign unique identifier codes to each activity, allowing their subsequent reconfiguration by business unit, core business process, attribute, or other activity center.

This develops an "as-is" activity model of your organization. It is common to do this by major business unit first and by core business process later when you have information on resources consumed by the activities.

Developing this model is a job for a team of senior managers who are familiar with all aspects of an organization. How long they spend doing this task depends on the your organization's complexity. The model should be considered in draft form, then circulated among business unit managers for comments and sign-off. At that point, you'll have a basic structure of business operations agreed upon by everyone in your organization.

Developing cost models

This step plugs cost information into the activity model. Details of the procedures used are discussed in Chapter 6. Here we will summarize each task.

Collect and assign cost data to activities. Salaries and benefits are the largest portion of operations costs of most government organizations. Organizations estimate this labor cost by activity, using methods such as observation, interviews, and employee surveys. Nonlabor costs such as materials, supplies, and facilities use are directly traced to an activity as much as possible. Costs that cannot otherwise be traced to an activity are allocated by an agreed-upon formula.

Aggregate cost data by business unit processes. This is the sum of all activity costs within a specific process inside a business unit. Labor costs by activity should be equivalent to the annual staff budget of that business unit. Many nonlabor costs will vary, however, because they have been traced directly to the processes instead of allocated by some general (and often misleading) formula.

Aggregate cost data by core business processes. You do this using activity centers that correspond to the processes, as discussed in Chapter 5.

Validate results. Before analyzing the information developed in the previous steps, validate it once more with executives and business unit managers. We recommend that you conduct individual briefings on the results for business unit heads and give them several days to make adjustments to improve accuracy.

Conducting analyses

As discussed in Chapter 6, there are a variety of analyses you can conduct using the activity and cost data you have collected. These include calculating product or service costs; comparing the costs of serving different groups of customers; cost-of-quality; and value analysis.

Except for value analysis, these studies are ideal tasks for line managers and employees aided by your team members and other specialists. Adding them to the initiative at this point will provide additional insight into the analyses and help expand your cadre of people who understand activity methods and benefits.

Value analysis is an exception because it is an intensive short-term effort that requires people with cross-functional experience, special training, and extreme objectivity. The best way to do this is to assign the task to a team of people who are familiar with the activity under examination. Ideally, these will be people who work in the activities. Their results should in turn be reviewed and validated by senior managers who "own" the activities. This ensures that the results will be credible to people in the activities and the entire organization.

Developing performance measures

This step identify outputs and annual volumes for each process, then develops process performance measures. The measures establish a baseline with which to assess process improvements, benchmark external processes, and develop better performance tracking systems. Again, these measures must be validated by managers of the activities involved.

Presenting findings

The final step in an ABC assessment is when you present your findings and they are accepted.

Figure 7-2
Keys to Successful
Presentation of
ABC Results

The two keys to a successful presentation of activity information are (1) no surprises and (2) commitment to action.

It is good to make the final presentation a special event. Invite all the key players: executives and managers who took part in the study. This way everyone will see who participated and that this was a serious undertaking. Any questions asked can be answered by someone in the room.

When presenting results to executives and managers, remember that ABC information can be surprising. You want to avoid surprises, though, because they might be too surprising (and maybe embarrassing) to some people. If you validated the findings of individual work units or activities with their managers, they won't be surprised at the final meeting. It is also a good idea to individually brief each change sponsor and other executive on the highlights of the findings before the final presentation. Note their questions and comments, and incorporate them into the final presentation.

Most people at the presentation will have already seen the details of findings on particular work units or activities, so this final presentation should focus on the "big picture" that pulls everything together. Spend extra time preparing for this meeting and have each presenter practice his or her part. Graphics such as bar charts, pie charts, and high-level process maps are excellent ways to present overviews of activity data. Many executives prefer these to reams of small-print reports. Make sure to have those reports ready because people will ask questions that you should answer immediately. After all, the purpose of ABC is to provide quick access to detailed information.

Cost Management and Controls

Internal control is the process by which management and other stakeholders obtain reasonable assurance that specified objectives are achieved. Controls can be operations-, finance and compliance-related. They must be designed into the organization, not built on top of it. Typically, this can be done by identifying control objectives and gaps between objectives and existing controls, preparing recommendations for enhancing controls, and "cross-walking" controls to activities and processes, as shown in Figure 7-3. Linking controls to activities and processes is critical to ensuring that a common language is used in establishing an effective control environment.

Figure 7-3
Relationship of
Controls
Objectives in ABC

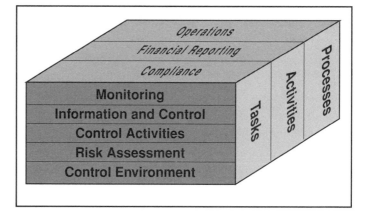

Many factors establish the groundwork for an effective control environment. These include policies and procedures, value systems, empowered employees who are responsible and accountable for work processes, sharing business information, top-down and bottom-up communication channels, and an organizational structure that supports operations.

ABC, through the dissemination of organization-wide process and activity information, is a catalyst in laying the groundwork for an effective control environment. Activity information, available to each employee, provides individuals with the knowledge necessary to manage work processes. Once empowered with this knowledge, employees no longer hesitate to make decisions and be held accountable for work processes. ABC provides employees with a common language for communications. In addition, ABC models are usually structured in no more than three to five layers, supporting the movement toward flatter organizational management.

Risk assessment

Organizations face operations-, finance-, or compliance-related risks, and any business process or activity is a candidate for effective risk management. The risks include incorrectly calculating the cost of an investment, failure to detect major problems in processes, and product or service failures in the field.

Risk management should be regarded as establishing objectives for a given activity or process. Using performance measures, ABC offers assistance by tracking activity volumes, costs, and attributes. For example, activity attributes such as cost-of-quality categories identify the resources invested in prevention activities versus inspection activities and quantify the cost of internal versus external failure. This provides indicators of the efficiency and effectiveness of quality systems.

Other attribute reports help mitigate risk. For example, cycle time reports on activities such as financial statement preparation assist in examining the timeliness of reporting activities. Activity reports can also be generated to examine the compliance framework and the effectiveness of compliance processes.

Control activities

Control activities are the policies and procedures that ensure that an organization's strategy and management directives are carried out at all levels. ABC reports provide controls with the visibility needed to ensure that they are accessible and usable by employees. Control reviews can be mapped against the processes and activities of the organization. Activity reports can be created that combine individual activities linked to a specific control factor, such as compliance with a regulatory standard. This mapping is critical in evaluating the effect of controls on activities.

Monitoring

Monitoring activities should be an ongoing task. Controls, because they are built into the work processes of the enterprise, must also be routinely monitored.

ABC systems are updated on a quarterly or semi-annual basis. Controls should typically be reviewed at this time as well. Control reports should not be constructed independent of ABC systems; once control reviews become integral to ABC, the need for separate reports no longer exists.

ABC Information Systems Planning

At first, you can get by with special studies and a separate data system for ABC, but to make using it easy and routine ABC must become part of your organization's information systems. This is essential if you want ABC to be part of normal managerial and financial decision-making.

Only a few years ago automated ABC systems were few, hard to use, and often quite primitive. Today, as ABC is incorporated in mainstream financial and management reporting, these systems are becoming more common, user friendly, and sophisticated. In fact, the availability of better systems technology has accelerated the adoption of ABC.

We know of no organization, government or private, that has completely scrapped its existing financial information system in favor of one that uses only an ABC approach. There are legal reasons for this, including statutory financial reporting requirements, and practical ones, because ABC is not appropriate for every type of financial analysis. The current trend is to integrate ABC data collection, analysis, and reporting into existing systems.

What should an integrated ABC system allow you to do?

At a minimum, you want an information system that allows you to identify and track activity performance measures, as discussed in Chapter 8; generate cost and other reports on activities and processes by their different attributes; and aggregate activities and their costs into different processes, as with activity centers. Advanced systems should enable you to generate data to be used in process simulation analysis. All ABC information systems should be flexible enough to quickly incorporate changes in activities.

> **Process simulation:** Using computer software to run trials of as-is and to-be models of activities and processes to test "what-if" assumptions about continuous improvement and reengineering.

It is beyond the scope of this book to provide you with the detailed steps involved in introducing an organization-wide ABC information system. Instead, we include an overview of the initial step, systems requirement analysis, in this chapter because doing it correctly will help to ensure success in subsequent steps.

Systems requirement analysis

You begin developing an ABC system by conducting a systems requirement analysis (SRA). The SRA determines the new system's requirements and identifies the best alternatives for its introduction. After completing an SRA, you will need to do more detailed system design, but the SRA provides the foundation for this.

Sound SRA approaches have three phases: project planning, analysis, and reporting, as discussed below.

Project planning. This phase begins with a meeting with the project sponsor, who is the senior manager in charge of introducing the system. The sponsor selects a project team and team leader, who usually include line managers who will use ABC information for their decisions. Accountants and information technology specialists should also participate. The sponsor prepares a team charter that spells out the objectives and scope of the project; all team members must agree with the charter. A sample charter from one government agency is shown below:

> **Objectives:** To analyze the organization's processes and the work they create; users' needs and systems; and attributes such as cost, value added/non-value added, cost-of-quality, and controls, in order to prepare a feasibility study for implementing an ABC information system. As part of the study and as pilot projects, ABC models will be developed for [core business process #1] and [core business process #2]. The results from the pilot projects will be incorporated into the study's recommendations.

> **Scope:** The feasibility study will address an organization-wide ABC implementation.

To meet the objectives, the team develops a detailed work plan that provides an initial vision of the ABC system and a route map that identifies, by implementation phase, the requisite products and documentation. In preparing the work plan, the team:

- Identifies and refines the expectations of system users and stakeholders

- Establishes a structure for reporting and delivery

- Reviews existing financial systems planning documentation

- Reviews other relevant financial systems documentation, such as data models and ABC studies

- Conducts a pilot study, if needed.

This review establishes a strategic vision of the ABC system that ensures that the rest of the project will go in the right direction to achieve the vision. The vision also focuses management attention on ABC requirements, strategic capabilities, and major information technology issues.

Conducting a pilot study is optional, but taking this step helps ensure success. Pilots provide specific and detailed information for planning and design and enable potential system users to understand both existing and future system capabilities. Thus, a pilot can be a catalyst for generating acceptance of ABC itself, as well as the new ABC system. As discussed in Chapter 12, pilots also provide information for making immediate process improvements, which should be made as part of this initial effort.

Analysis. The analysis phase leads to determining requirements for the new system and identifies the best alternative for system implementation. The systems requirement document uses process and data modeling techniques to analyze and report the business or functional requirements that will be supported by the ABC system.

The team does not initially distinguish between manual and automated components of the system or dictate how automation might be done, but once requirements are established, the team can begin to explore implementation alternatives. These may include off-the-shelf software versus customized software, or the extent to which data collection and analysis will be automated. Before making a recommendation the team considers the effect of alternative solutions in terms of resources and risks. In the case of off-the-shelf solutions, there are now many commercial ABC packages available.

Reporting. Finally, the team consolidates its findings in a detailed feasibility report and presents it to senior management. The final report should include:

- A "short list" of implementation alternatives

- Recommended best alternative

- Inventory of available data sources and a "gap analysis" of what is available versus what is needed

- A list of potential users and uses of ABC information

- A change management plan for the introduction of the new system (see Chapter 11).

The report should also address subsequent analytical steps, including the system design specifications, which provide the detailed design information necessary to build ABC into an existing information system.

Summary

Understanding where you want ABC to take your organization is important when you consider any activity-based information project. Simply put, the purpose of ABC information is to enable managers and employees to make better decisions about how to change operations. Unfortunately, some organizations lose sight of this objective and end up with "lots of great data" but no results. Thus, no ABC project should be undertaken without clear knowledge of who will use the information, for what purpose, and in what manner.

New Principles from Chapter 7

ABC Projects, Controls, and Information Systems

Old Rule or Practice	New Principle or Practice

Old Rule or Practice	New Principle or Practice

PART III

ACTIVITY-BASED MANAGEMENT

Chapter

8

About Activity-Based Management

- Most organizations have difficulty making major changes in operations. Activity-Based Management is based on enabling organizations to change.

- Activity-Based Management helps create flexible structure and capacity, which allow an organization to continuously prepare for change.

- In Activity-Based Management, strategic goals and critical success factors can be directly linked to all levels of operation.

- Activity budgets are based on the dynamics of processes and provide several perspectives on proposed actions. This makes them tools for change, instead of static documents on spending.

"One thing that is new is the prevalence of newness, the changing scale and scope of change itself, so that the world alters as we walk in it."

—J. Robert Oppenheimer,
Director of the Manhattan Project

In a world full of change, organizations capable of changing will survive. Most government organizations are having a hard time changing. They try, but with the unfortunate—and fatal—goal of building newer, better, more stable operations. The fatal flaw? Stability. It is not going to happen now or in the future, and probably was a false assumption in the past.

That's why Activity-Based Management is more about flexibility than stability, more about dynamics than the status quo. In this chapter, we outline the characteristics of Activity-Based Management that give it the ability to change.

Figure 8-1 shows those characteristics. You've just read several chapters on activity-based costing, and Chapter 3 showed how it integrates with quality management. Here we will look at the others.

Figure 8-1
Characteristics of
Activity-Based
Management

> - Activity-based costing
>
> - Management structure built around core business processes
>
> - Top-down and bottom-up emphasis on improvement
>
> - Activity budgeting
>
> - Flexible capacity
>
> - Quality management principles and practices

Management Structure Built Around Core Business Processes

An organization that follows the principles of Activity-Based Management structures its operations along process lines. This structure can be made a formal part of the organization chart, as the Internal Revenue Service (IRS) has done, or it can simply be way of running the organization (even a though the chart remains as before). Either way, the intent is the same: manage by process, not by boxes on a chart.

Core business processes at the IRS

In 1992 the IRS divided all its business into five core business systems (CBS): *managing accounts, informing and educating, ensuring compliance, resourcing,* and *value tracking* (see Figure 4-5). Each CBS is the same as a core business process. The three italicized CBS' above are "customer touch" operations, and the other two are support operations.

This arrangement recognizes that many, if not most, IRS frontline personnel often work in cross-functional processes that transcend traditional department boundaries. It reflects how work gets done in the field, at service centers, and at headquarters.

One IRS manager told us, "This allows us to begin to blend the jobs and skill sets of people while we start merging the processes from different CBS'. For example, a tax case used to move from functional department to functional department, with many delays and hand-off errors. Now we're successfully trying out case management in which one agent handles all aspects of a single case. You can't do that in an organization with rigid functional boundaries."

Another IRS manager added, "We've made it clear that the 'customer touch' CBS' call the shots for support CBS'. For example, our old marketing research group had its own agenda, without sponsors from the rest of the IRS. They would say, 'Here, look at this. Isn't it great? Why don't you do something with it?' Now all our market research has sponsors from our internal customers."

"We are, of course, doing some more visible restructuring, such as going from 70 telephone inquiry centers to 20," said a senior manager. "Also, our automation and telecommunication projects are making fundamental changes to the way we do business. What you don't see is that these physical changes are being guided by the way our CBS structure forces us to look at processes. Before we developed the CBS approach no one paid attention to our attempts to introduce Activity-Based Management. Now everyone is interested because it's the way we do business."

Role of the functional department

Most companies and agencies are organized as in the functional chart shown in Figure 8-2. This arrangement evolved from military and industrial models in the 19th and early 20th centuries. It is a functional model: each box on the chart is tied to a specific function such as planning, production, distribution, etc. Each function hires experts in its professional specialty, and most people rise through the ranks of their profession.

Figure 8-2

Traditional
Organizational
Chart

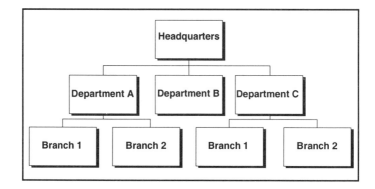

Some organizations have proposed doing away with functional departments entirely. Instead, their staffs would form teams organized around the value chain that begins with customer requests for service and ends when those requests are fulfilled. Each team thus has its own production, accounting, personnel, planning, and other functions. This is a seductive alternative, but it has serious problems.

First, functional specialists in these situations tend to apply what they have learned about their specialty in the past, but they do not learn new things about it. Although they become better generalists because of their exposure to other disciplines on a team, this does not foster leading-edge technical knowledge of a specialty. Functional departments provide a means for this continued learning, both formally (in-house seminars and sponsored outside education) and informally (interaction with peers).

Second, where do these specialists go at the end of a project or a product's life cycle, or when they want to advance up the organizational ladder or work on something else? They need a career and a "home" offered by membership in a functional department.

Functions and departments are part of organizations that follow Activity-Based Management but are seen as supporting the operation of processes, not as quasi-independent work units.

Organizing around projects at the shipyards

For example, consider how the Naval shipyards have restructured around core business processes while maintaining functional departments. Until recently, the direct labor of overhaul work at the shipyards was controlled by the heads of functional departments or shops such as pipefitting, welding, electrical work, carpentry, etc. Each department head decided what types of workers and how many to send to a job. Work often occurred out of sequence. For example, electrical components were installed that later had to be removed to do other tasks. The number of workers a department head sent to a job frequently corresponded to the number of people without any work to do at the time. This usually meant too many hands for too little work.

In the new system, a single project manager has responsibility and authority for all operations on the core business process of overhauling a vessel from the time it is planned until it returns to the fleet. These managers "rent" from the departments the type and number of specialists and equipment they need for jobs and control these specialists on the job. One program manager told us, "I want nothing more or less than the resources I need for a job, and I'm constantly looking for ways to do the work for less. This starts at the planning and estimating stage, when we figure out a budget and work plan. My team and I do the planning, and we live with the results. You had better believe I am motivated to make improvements and save money."

Similarities and differences in the IRS and shipyards approaches

Temporary versus permanent structure: At shipyards, the activity structure is built around the individual ship overhaul project. This is a temporary structure that disappears after the project is over. One reason for this is that each yard does relatively few overhauls, but these projects are large, complex, and often require a customized arrangement of activities. This calls for a flexible structure. On the other hand, the IRS carries out millions of standard transactions a year, and requires a more permanent activity structure.

Role of the process owner: In both the IRS and the shipyards, process managers are responsible for controlling and improving their processes. Because of this, they are sometimes called *process owners.*

At the IRS the highest level of process owners are the heads of major departments. Each is responsible for specific cross-functional processes that take place mainly within his or her department boundaries but that have parts that are done in other departments.

At the shipyards the process owners are project managers. They are responsible for making improvements to cross-functional processes during their projects; they do this by working with department managers, who are responsible for managing and improving those parts of a ship overhaul that occur within the boundaries of their departments.

Whichever arrangement you choose, appointing process owners is essential for effective activity management. This practice helps your organization avoid compartmentalizing its operations into the artificial boundaries of functions and departments.

Functions and departments. Functional units and departments still remain in both the shipyards and the IRS. They serve valuable purposes, as was discussed earlier, but the actual work of both organizations is now designed around cross-functional processes. At the IRS the functional inputs of some work are being focused through reengineering into individual employee processes such as case management. Increased use of information technology, such as artificial intelligence systems, will accelerate this practice in all organizations.

Top-down and Bottom-up Improvement

In Chapter 3 an IRS manager noted that the organization's TQM effort had become largely a bottom-up effort. Activity-Based Management provided the means to make top-down improvements as well. Here we examine how effective performance measurement makes it possible to have it both ways.

Measuring for action

ABC measurement has this central premise: "Ultimately, all performance measures must be linked to activities." Unless this link is made, you will not be able to take action to improve. Why? Because improvement comes from changing the way work is done, and activities are how work is done in an organization. This is true for both existing activities and those that must be newly created to meet customer expectations.

This is also true for measures of both efficiency and effectiveness. For example, ABC readily measures an activity's efficiency by using internal information on cost, cycle time, errors, and so on. ABC does not, however, readily measure effectiveness, such as degree of customer satisfaction. Instead, ABC defines the activity or process to be measured for effectiveness and shows its links to other parts of an organization.

Measuring what is important

Performance measurement means giving feedback on activities and outputs. Activity-Based Management organizations provide this feedback to all levels of operations. The framework for doing this is shown in Figure 8-3. At the senior management level measures are tied to customer and mission requirements. These are not just today's requirements: they look toward the future, when demand and environment will be different. That is why executives recast current and future requirements into strategic goals.

Figure 8-3
Performance
Measurement and
Feedback

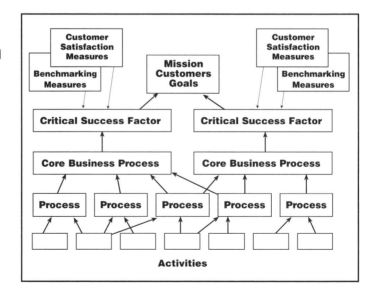

Many organizations go further and translate requirements into strategic critical success factors (CSFs). CSFs are those few areas that an organization absolutely must do right if it is to meet customer requirements. In various kinds of organizations, they may include:

- **Military depot.** Acquiring mission-critical materials quickly and cost-effectively

- **Economic development agency.** Evaluating complex information from diverse sources

- **Laboratory.** Safe handling of hazardous substances

- **Research grant agency.** Acquiring information on the state of the art in different subjects.

- **All government organizations.** Excellent stewardship of public funds and other resources, including usage, handling, and accounting.

Organizations create key performance indicators based on their CSFs. These are quantitative measures of efficiency and effectiveness: customer satisfaction, cost, cycle time, quality, desired or undesired events, degree of coverage of an area or target group, and so on. Many organizations will benchmark their performance against best-in-class results of outside organizations.

Critics of the CSF method say that it tends to be myopic because only a few areas of operations are measured and then usually only by their outcomes. Often, continue the critics, there are only vague links between a CSF indicator and operations performance measures. We agree that this is true in many CSF applications.

A CSF also is a core business process. As processes, CSFs are by definition linked to their constituent activities. This lets executives view CSF performance in aggregate or by activity, including the effect of support processes. For example, executives can quantify the total cost of core business process outputs (see Chapter 5) or their cost-of-quality (COQ, see Chapter 3). ABC makes it easier to benchmark the performance of similar processes in other organizations (see Chapter 5) or to focus on measuring internal or external customer satisfaction with a single process and its outputs.

Because they have performance pictures for several levels of a core business process, executives are better able to understand weaknesses and opportunities in operations. This leads to top-level improvement decisions informed by knowledge of what needs to change.

ABC by itself will not produce all the measures needed for all CSFs. Others include customer satisfaction, field performance, meeting established standards, and investment in innovation. ABC will, however, help develop many of the operations measures for activities that lead to these results.

Enabling people to control and improve operations

ABC's top-to-bottom, bottom-to-top measurement links mean that managers and employees can understand how their activities contribute to CSF performance. Thus, they can meet strategic goals by homing in on performance measures important to controlling and improving their specific operations. This helps everyone stay on the track leading to superior organizational performance.

Armed with activity maps and flowcharts, operations personnel can install measures at critical points in an activity. By studying cost drivers, ABC analyses, and results of such methods as statistical process control, they will understand what causes those measures to change.

Enhancing and managing bottom-up improvement

Not all improvements need to be directed at core business processes and CSFs. Managers and employees must be allowed to enhance operations secondary to an organization's mission, but, like top executives, their improvement decisions must be informed by hard, objective performance measurements. This ensures a healthier bottom-up improvement approach.

Improvement needs performance measurement, too

"Improving" is itself an activity that should be managed like all others. It also has a set of performance measures:

- The number of employee suggestions made, the percent accepted and implemented, the average time needed to take action on a suggestion, and the costs of running the suggestion program and its financial benefit to an organization

- The costs (training, labor, equipment, and facilities) of process improvement initiatives as well as the financial or other returns on this investment.

Many organizations do not collect this information and so cannot effectively manage improvement. This is as true at the top as it is the bottom. By treating improvement as an activity, or even as a core business process, top management is able to understand and enhance it.

"Sizing" to Meet Changes in Work Load

In this section, we show how ABC and Activity-Based Management help a public organization to make sound decisions about increasing or decreasing its capacity to produce goods and services.

Defining work load and sizing

Demand for government goods and services often exceeds available resources, which is why lawmakers establish limits on what public organizations can provide to their customers. These limits are an agency's *work load* or the amount of goods or services that lawmakers expect a government organization to produce over a given period.

When work load is expected to increase or decrease over the long term, an organization must alter its capacity to handle the change. For most government organizations, this usually means increasing or decreasing the *size* of their work force. Such sizing also can apply to equipment, facilities, and contractor support.

Conventional approaches to sizing

Some government organizations react to changes in work load with across the board budget or staff cuts or increases for all their departments and functions. For example, all department directors may be ordered to find ways to trim 10 percent from their budget. As we discuss more in the next chapter on restructuring, this often leaves some activities too fat, and others dangerously lean.

Often, this is the result of inadequate cost and activity information needed to n - ke correct decisions about the impact of work load changes on staffing at the department or cost center levels. Most organizations know how much is being spent by their departments, but do not know the outputs of that spending. For example, as shown in the top half of Figure 8-4, most accounting systems will tell you that you spend $1 million a year in a purchasing department. But they do not tell you how many purchase orders are being processed now, nor how many will be needed if work load changes. In this situation, you may be forced to raise or reduce arbitrarily the purchasing department's budget.

You would take a different approach to the situation under Activity-Based Management. You already would have a cost model of your organization that links outputs to activities and activities to the resources they consume, such as that shown in the bottom half of Figure 8-4. With the model, you would use volume measures, activity drivers, and cost drivers to find how resources consumed by each activity in the organization might vary under a new work load scenario.

For example, if a shipyard knows that it will have ten fewer ships of a certain type to overhaul three years from now, the yard's cost model will show how many fewer outputs like purchase orders will be needed for each overhaul project. If a contract audit organization expects to increase the number of audits it conducts for a certain type of contract, its cost model will show the effect of the change not only on the number of auditors needed, but also on the work load of the personnel department that supports those auditors.

At the shipyard, fewer purchase orders will decrease the work load of the purchasing department. This does not mean that the staff or budget of each purchasing activity should be reduced by the same percentage, however. For example, an ABC cost model would show that unit level activities such as updating files on purchase orders are sensitive to changes in work load. Batch level activities, such as periodically auditing a sample of processed purchase orders, are less sensitive to work load changes. Activities that sustain the purchasing department, such as designing staff training courses, are the least sensitive and may not change at all unless the organization eliminates the use of purchase orders.

ABC cost model information therefore helps a purchasing director develop sound recommendations to top management about how to adjust the staffing levels of each activity in the department in response to a change in the number of purchase orders. Further, the director can defend his or her recommendations with objective data.

This does not mean that managers in an Activity-Based Management organization only use ABC data to inform their decisions about sizing. A manager's experience in working with his or her activities is also important. What ABC provides is another view of the dynamics of activities to which a manager applies that experience.

Figure 8-4
Two Views of
Purchase Order
Process

Line-Item Budget View

Salaries	$742,538
Computer	91,500
Telecommunications	30,880
Supplies	34,115
Facilities	81,373
Total	$980,407
Full-timeequivalents (FTEs)	18.6

ABC View

Activity	Volume	Output	FTEs	Total Cost	Unit Cost	Labor Cost	Computer	Telecom-munication	Supplies	Facilities
Process new purchase orders (p.o.)	70,000	Completed p.o.	7.8	$407,167	$5.82	$303,333	$35,000	$17,500	$14,000	$37,333
Update p.o. files	210,000	Updated p.o.	5.8	322,000	1.53	227,500	52,500	10,500	10,500	21,000
Answer audit queries	50	Query answered	0.7	33,533	670.67	30,333	0	0	0	3,200
Design training courses	3	Courses designed	0.1	8,287	2,762.22	5,547	0	0	2,100	640
Conduct training courses	270	Days of training	0.2	12,900	47.78	6,825	0	0	6,075	0
Supervise p.o. operations	16	Employees supervised	2.0	120,160	7,510.00	104,000	2,000	1,440	720	12,000
Other administrative/ clerical work		No unit measure	2.0	76,360		65,000	2,000	1,440	720	7,200
TOTAL			18.6	$980,407		$742,538	$91,500	$30,880	$34,115	$81,373

Sizing and cross-functional processes

Let's not forget that processes such as those used for purchase orders are cross-functional. Someone outside a purchasing department has to write a requisition before a
purchase order is handled by that department. A reduction
in purchase orders means fewer requisitions, so there are
opportunities outside the purchasing department to make
adjustments to work load. An ABC cost model that treats
purchasing as a cross-functional process will help to find
these opportunities.

Activity Budgeting

At a 1994 Indianapolis community meeting, citizens and
media reporters gathered around an amazing document. It
told them not only how much the City would spend on road
repairs and maintenance, but precisely what they would get
for that portion of their taxes. The document included the
full cost, derived from ABC, of each type of service the City
planned to deliver: how many linear feet of deteriorated
curbs would be repaired or replaced (1,500 feet, at $23.50 per
foot), 14,000 road signs averaging $30.24 each—it was a bud-
get anyone could understand.

But it was more than a budget. The document was a
promise to citizens to increase productivity and efficiency.
How many budget documents do you know that have
phrases like "crews will improve response time by 25 to 50
percent" and "for more efficient use of tax dollars?"
Moreover, if you challenged those types of statements, few
government organizations could immediately give you the
details of how they were going to improve.

"We call it our 'popular' budget," a financial officer at the
City Department of Capital Asset Management told us.
"Before 1994, we gave citizens a line-item budget. We would
spend hours explaining it, but many would still not understand. With the popular budget, what you see is what you
get, plain and simple. Citizens tell us they love it."

Behind that budget is solid and detailed information of each activity done by the Department, precisely how much resources each activity consumes, accurate unit costs of production, and what drives the costs. "It is a better way for Department managers to look at a budget," the financial officer continued. "That's because the core of our budgetary process are the activity and cost models built from everyone participating in activity mapping and costing. We still prepare line-item budgets required by statute, but we use an activity-based budget."

Traditional budgeting

A former Secretary of Defense once said, "The budget evolved from a management tool into an obstacle to management."[16] Think about your existing budgetary process. What percentage of the people in your organization are involved in that process, and how much time do they spend doing it? One study showed that, in 10 large energy, transportation, and banking companies, an average of five percent of all staff employees were engaged full-time in budgeting activities![17] This is frightening, when you consider that the budgeting process for most organizations would be classified as non-value added.

Next think about how useful budget documents really are to managing your organization or operation. Do they tell you why resources are being consumed in certain ways? The effectiveness of that resource use? The true unit cost of delivering goods and services? Your budget probably shows the amount of spending, by line item, that will go to different programs and to support your whole organization. That's why most government budgets gather dust on shelves after they're approved.

Activity-Based Management has several approaches to budgeting, each giving you a different view of an organization. These include activity, product or service, customer or customer group, and strategic views. When you have digested and used this information, it all folds back into the usual budget format. Best of all, this is easy information to generate if you practice ABC.

Different budgetary views

Activity budgets are simply large-scale activity and cost models based on past resource usage; projected demand; and assumptions about improvement, technology, and other factors. Using the activity centers discussed in Chapter 5, they can focus only on major processes or go all the way down to the activity level. They show what resources an activity or process consumed during previous periods and proposed consumption in the future. They also identify what outputs are now or will be flowing from one activity to others, so that executives can understand who will be doing what for whom and for how much.

This type of budget includes activity- and process-level performance measures, cost drivers, activity drivers, and the cost of products, services, and serving different customers. Many show whether an activity or process is value added or non-value added. With this information, executives and managers can ask—and have immediate answers to—questions about performance improvement and the impact of changes in work load or technology.

Product budgets show the proposed cost of an organization's products and services. They are created by identifying which activities will produce these outputs and the amount of resources they will consume doing it. This allows cost comparisons with benchmarked products and services.

Customer budgets show proposed costs of providing services to individual customers or groups of customers. Such analysis helps executives determine if a disproportionate share of resources is being devoted to any one customer or group and the reasons why. By using activity centers such as "customer support services," these budgets lead to questions about how such costs can be reduced.

Strategic budgets propose resource usage by processes linked to an organization's long-range plans and operations strategies. These budgets can relate to core business processes linked to CSFs, capital investment, and changes in basic strategies for serving the public (i.e., "steering more and rowing less," as the National Performance Review would say).

Flexibility in budgeting

For every view above, budgets can be disaggregated into different categories, such as "environmental protection," "training," and "facilities maintenance." All you need to do is create an activity center to show what activities these categories will involve and how their resource consumption will change under your proposals.

The sources of change in resource consumption during a budget period can be more easily identified with activity costing than with traditional accounting's budget variance reports. If major changes occur, their impact on the total budget is easier to understand with activity and cost models geared to that budget.

Summary

Activity-Based Management's greatest strength is to make change happen in desired directions. It enables executives to take charge of change through better understanding of how an organization operates and consumes resources. Moreover, the executives do not have to micromanage to gain strategic goals. Instead, everyone in the organization understands where his or her activity stands in relation to strategic goals and critical success factors. This helps focus improvement efforts on what is important to mission and customers.

New Principles from Chapter 8

About Activity-Based Management

Old Rule or Practice	New Principle or Practice

Old Rule or Practice	New Principle or Practice

Chapter

9

Restructuring

- Most attempts to downsize have eliminated jobs but not work, meaning major problems for organizations.

- Activity-Based Management provides the information and methods to sensibly restructure an organization.

- The greatest opportunities for restructuring in government are to be found among support functions.

- Restructuring should be done to fit the major cross-functional processes that deliver value to customers.

- Organizations must become skilled in restructuring as a process because a turbulent environment will require continual adjustment.

"When most companies reorganize, usually they focus on the formal structure of the organization—the boxes in the organizational chart. . . Rarely do senior executives contemplate changing the basic processes and behaviors by which a company operates."
—Paul Allaire,
Xerox Chairman and CEO

In Activity-Based Management, restructuring an organization means altering its size, shape, work processes, and communications systems to meet new requirements or opportunities. This is different from "downsizing," a term associated with massive layoffs. Nor is it "rightsizing," which implies a change in size but not in the other three factors. And it is more than "reorganizing," or simply shuffling boxes around on an organizational chart.

Let's take an extended look at how a government organization undergoing major work load reductions is doing more than simply downsizing. Later on, you'll see how other organizations with the opposite problem—growing work loads—restructure to become more effective.

Restructuring Support Functions

In the early 1990s, the U.S. Navy ran eight shipyards to repair and overhaul its surface ships and submarines. By the end of the decade, there will be at most only five, and possibly fewer. The key reason is the downsizing of the U.S. Naval fleet from nearly 580 to a possible low of 300 vessels. Also, changes to vessel design and maintenance strategies mean that ships need less shipyard-based servicing.

About 80 percent of the cost of a vessel's overhaul goes for direct and indirect labor. Blue-collar line departments do most of the direct labor at the waterfront, such as welding, wiring, and pipe fitting. Support departments, staffed by both blue- and white-collar workers, do indirect work such as planning, materials management, security, personnel, accounting, and administration.

Visibility of support functions

Determining the size of a direct labor force is often a fairly straightforward exercise. If you know you will over-haul five vessels of a certain type, then you have a good idea of the number and type of waterfront people you will use. According to one shipyard commanding officer, "Direct labor is very visible: you can see it happen. Many support processes are less visible: you don't see 'planning' and 'administration' happen the same way you see someone turn a wrench. Also, most senior executives come from line departments, so they don't understand how support depart-ment processes work."

Because few executives know where to begin to reduce sup-port functions, most simply assume that they are all "too fat," do across-the-board budget and personnel cuts, and leave it to support managers to decide where to slim down. Says one shipyard executive, "The result of this attitude is to transform large, bloated, and inefficient bureaucracies into smaller, bloated, and inefficient bureaucracies. You end up still too fat in some areas, but dangerously thin in others."

Support functions not planned

A close look at a support department can reveal a disheart-ening tangle of inefficient work flows, redundancies, and much unneeded work. Why? Unlike many direct labor pro-cesses, few support processes grew by design. Instead, they evolved by reacting to the requirements of the day, which might have evaporated the day after. For example, in a sin-gle process the following might occur:

- A manager may have once demanded to review all reports related to a certain subject. Long after he retired, those reports continue to be checked by his replace-ments, even though the need for this has passed (if it even existed to begin with).

- More cost may have been added by a strict interpretation of an external acquisition regulation. The result: $30 purchases are treated the same as $10,000 buys.

- New technology ended the need for an inspection activity to detect errors, but the activity remains because no one thought to eliminate it.

The result is a hodgepodge that continues to proliferate every year, unnoticed and unchecked by top management. This problem led six of the shipyards to use ABC to learn more about their support departments before deciding how to restructure them.

Mapping and analyzing the value added by support processes

Using activity analysis, each shipyard mapped how support functions operated, what they cost, who worked in them, and where this work took place. Each yard also conducted value analysis. Among the findings:

- **Location of work.** Remember the shipyard job order planning process we mentioned in Chapter 1? At least half of the resources devoted to it went to line and support departments outside the planning department. Fewer vessels to be overhauled meant less demand for the services of the planning department, and for related work done elsewhere. This latter opportunity for savings would have been missed without activity analysis.

- **Unneeded work.** More than half of the resources devoted to support functions went to nonmandatory, non-value added work. Said one executive, "The magnitude of this showed us we could expect to substantially reduce the costs of support functions by eliminating non-value added activities. This meant less work, which was fortunate since we were going to have fewer people around after downsizing."

- **Opportunities for centralizing.** Activity data revealed that support departments were spending too much time on tasks such as travel vouchers, W-2 forms, savings bonds, and so on. One shipyard decided to centralize these into a "one-stop-people-shop" at the waterfront, where all employees could come with questions and get forms and assistance. Data analysis helped to figure out the shop's staffing level and equipment needs and verified the types of activities required to support it. The result was better, more accurate service because the staff were specially trained in their work. Fewer staff hours were needed in this centralized set-up than when the work was done in the departments.

- **Appropriate staffing.** Activity data were used to calculate the staffing requirements of a restructured administrative services department at one shipyard. In reviewing the data, executives found that the pay grade of most of the department's employees was higher than normally required for the work they did. The restructured department now has fewer people at lower salary levels.

- **Politics.** Activity data helped executives to circumvent the usual politics involved in restructuring. For example, some astute managers with good lobbying skills had positioned themselves to get more job slots than their departments needed. One demanded 80 more people if his department was to take on new responsibilities. Top management pointed to where the data showed that he had too many people shuffling papers already, and hinted that he could transfer them over to some real work. That ended that.

In summary, Activity-Based Management helped Naval shipyards to better understand their support functions and to make wise decisions about their restructuring. Now that support processes and activities are visible, mapped, and measured, it will be easier to apply process improvement methods to them.

Consolidating Support Services

While the shipyards conducted an activity analysis their headquarters studied the benefit and feasibility of centralizing some of their support functions. This meant moving some support activities from the yards to one or two central locations, leaving behind those that had to be done locally. The reasons included the following:

- Information technology, especially in communications, meant that each shipyard did not need to have a full support staff on site to guarantee prompt service

- Centralizing some support activities might save money, so that more required maintenance could be done for the same price as before.

All six shipyards used a common classification and coding system during their activity analysis. "We asked the shipyards to use this information to come up with a plan for shifting some of their support work to a central organization," a senior headquarters manager told us. "We put together a team of representatives from each of the eight shipyards, and gave them the activity data from the six that had developed it. Also, we gave them a forecast of the number and type of overhauls and other work that would be required over the next several years. Then we asked them, 'How much of what type of support work will you need, and where should it take place?'"

The team divided into eight subteams with new members, each responsible for one of the eight shipyard business functions (see Figure 9-1). Using activity information, they first determined the amount of support services required for each of the overhauls the shipyards could expect. They then reviewed the activities to see which could be done at a remote site and which had to be done at or near the waterfront work areas.

Provide material support
Define, estimate, plan, schedule, and forecast work
Manage work execution at the waterfront
Provide administrative and general management support
Manage and maintain equipment, facilities, and tools
Manage training programs
Administer information systems
Manage safety and environment

Figure 9-1
Shipyard Core
Business
Processes

They found that in many cases more than half of a support process could be done outside a shipyard. Said the headquarters manager, "This means we can achieve some economies of scale at a central location. For example, if a yard now employs 14 engineers in a support activity, we might move six to a central location to do specialized work and planning for common processes, and leave two generalists on site to work on daily problems and needs. The other six would not be needed, due to reduced work load, better process design, and reuse of products such as engineering drawings. When we need to plan and estimate the cost of a specific overhaul, a team from the central and local sites can meet face-to-face or electronically to do the work."

"None of these decisions were obvious," she continued. "The teams did not take it for granted that something or someone could move. To win support for this out in the field, you have to be thorough and objective in your considerations. And it helps to put some of the best people in your field sites in charge of developing the recommendations— this encourages buy-in."

She concludes: "I don't think this would have worked if we set out looking for money savings alone, though. However, if you set out to be more effective, usually you end up saving money."

Reasons for Restructuring

There always are reasons for government organizations to reorganize: for elected or appointed officials to have better control of operations; to consolidate weaker units with stronger ones; or simply to shake up complacent internal management structure. All are valid reasons, but none creates fundamental change processes.

On the other hand, restructuring an organization along process lines is prompted by the following factors:

- **Information technology.** New technology makes it possible to disperse decision-making to field sites, line employees, and even to customers' homes. Conversely, as with the shipyards, technology enables an organization to centralize activities that once had to be done in each field office.

- **Major changes in work load.** With the end of the Cold War, most defense programs are restructuring their operations to reflect a decreased amount of work. Civilian organizations such as the Social Security Administration have the opposite problem. As the population ages, the SSA faces increased demand.

- **Changing demographics.** There are 30,000 federal government offices scattered across the country, many established when America was rural and there were no telecommunications.[18] Some agencies, such as the U.S. Department of Agriculture, have started to close and consolidate their less-used offices.

- **Reengineering.** A nationwide system to deliver government benefits electronically, called for by the National Performance Review[19], would radically alter processes for delivering federal pensions, Social Security, unemployment insurance, Aid to Families and Dependent Children (AFDC), and other cash payments to citizens. Each agency involved will need to restructure its delivery services around new processes.

- **Mission changes.** At the same time that their Cold War business dries up, many defense facilities face a decades-long job of cleaning up hazardous waste at their sites. What was once a support process has turned into their main mission.

Finally, all too many government agencies have simply had their budgets cut due to general fiscal austerity. When these cuts exceed 10 percent of a previous year's budget, it means these agencies may need to restructure to be effective. Unfortunately, most do not. Instead, fewer of their people work the same old way, attempting—and usually failing—to do the same amount of work as before.

This takes its toll not only on service to citizens, but also on the physical and mental health of employees and managers. Since 1980, the average American work week has increased by about six hours. For managers, the increase is probably higher, according to most studies. Many develop what the Japanese call karoshi, "death by overwork," usually of a heart attack.[20]

How Should You Restructure?

Like the shipyards, every organization has to come up with its own unique answer to this question. Below, we offer some questions that lead to that answer, and show more examples of how Activity-Based Management helps to guide restructuring.

What business do we need or want to be in?

First, you have to know the business you are in right now. ABC helps you do this by identifying your products, services, and the activities that produce them. Next you determine where your resources are flowing—the percentage of your budget that is being consumed by each activity.

For example, the City of Indianapolis' Department of Public Works used ABC to identify its street maintenance activities and their costs. Then, using the portfolio matrix shown in Figure 9-2, they reviewed each activity based on its resource consumption and value to customers. The vertical axis shows how strongly the public values a particular activity, based on its visibility, citizen interest, and complaints. The size of the circles shows the relative costs of each service and their shading represents future demand and potential funding for each.

Figure 9-2 Portfolio Matrix – Indianapolis

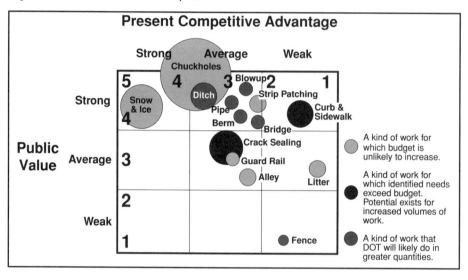

On the horizontal axis, the matrix shows the competitive advantage the Department has over other suppliers of the same type of activity. This describes whether they can do an activity better, faster, and with less cost than private contractors or other City departments. The data for this come from benchmarking these real or potential competitors.

Based on this analysis, the Department decided to stop using City crews for fencing and litter cleanup because they clearly could not do it as well as other organizations. Both activities were too small for heavy investment in internal improvements, neither was going to grow, and citizens did not give them much attention. It therefore made sense to contract out for fencing and turn over litter cleanup to another City department that did it better. "This type of analysis also helped us to understand our basic identity as a division," said a financial manager. "We are in the business of protecting and improving the physical infrastructure of the street system of the City. We want to concentrate on being competent in those things that are critical to that business. Cleaning litter and fencing are important, but they are not critical."

What about control?

Organizations traditionally use three methods of control: management, procedures, and rules. Restructuring is a good time to review the value that existing controls add to services and products.

Management. Organization planning specialist Robert M. Tomasko likes to point out that the Catholic Church has only three layers of management: priests, bishops, and the Pope.[21] Large public and private organizations have many more layers, mostly for control purposes, and this has been a problem.

Having many layers of management makes it much harder to get quick decisions, which are the key to flexibility in times of change. Many of the managers in those layers are simply "work watchers" who do not add value to the work with decisions and guidance. Others are "coordinators" who make sure one work unit knows what another is doing.

Information technology has started to change much of this. Today, information on operations, performance, and budgets is increasingly being captured at its source and automatically packaged for higher review. Better communications systems ensure that all people in an organization can be quickly contacted with new information, orders, and requests.

Another reason is the rise of self-managed teams. These "natural work groups" of employees plan, manage, execute, and report on work within their activities and coordinate with other activities in a process. Where once a supervisor was assigned to each activity, now one supervisor "coaches" several self-managed teams. Related to this is a drive toward allowing local operations more autonomy, which means less need for management from headquarters.

So several layers of management are no longer necessary to move information and orders up and down the corporate hierarchy—which is why those layers were created. This is the main reason that more than a million middle management jobs have disappeared from American industry in the past decade.

Another reason is that much of a manager's time is not spent managing. Review of the time middle managers spend on different activities reveals how much is devoted to actual management. You often find them spending all too much time on mundane administrative tasks that could be done by clerks or paraprofessionals. ABC labor surveys such as those discussed in Chapter 4 can be used to determine if this is true.

In government and some companies, the largest chunk of managers' time goes to professional and technical work in their functional specialty. This is due to a system in which career advancement and salary increases are possible only by rising through the ranks of management. Some organizations solve this problem by establishing dual-track career paths. One path is management; the other allows a professional to earn a salary equivalent to that just below executive status.

By subtracting the nonmanagerial work done by middle managers, you will find that you need fewer of them. Those that remain can focus on managing. The others can devote full time to professional and technical work, and may be happier because of this. As for managers whose only skills are work watching and coordinating, perhaps you would be better off without them.

Procedures. Control activities abound in government organizations and are most often the source of complaints about delays, bureaucracy, red tape, and extra cost. For example, a payables department may employ 30 people for $1 million a year. Their primary job is to prevent overpayment. To do this, they examine invoices, send copies to internal units who ordered and received the goods and to the accounting department to match orders and invoices, and verify things up and down the line. A close look at this activity will reveal that the clerks look at the same piece of paper five or six times.

Then, you discover that if you paid all invoices without going through this process, you might overpay by $30,000. Do citizens or your customers want to pay you $1 million to save $30,000? We doubt it. The point is, you have to strike a balance between the costs and benefits of any control activity. This begins by establishing its total costs, which include those internal to the activity and the work it causes for other activities. Activity-based costing will help you obtain this information.

Rules. Many support departments exist to write or enforce "rules" that dictate in excruciating detail how a process is to be run. If you get rid of the rules, you no longer need those departments. For example, the Naval Facilities Engineering Command (NAVFAC) once wrote thousands of pages of detailed regulations and task specifications on maintaining Navy facilities. "The book," as it was called, even specified how to paint a door—brush, primer, paint, and so on.

When NAVFAC leaders decided that good painters could figure this out themselves, they replaced "the book" with a short list of basic principles of good business. At Navy bases, customer satisfaction went up, costs went down, and maintenance employees began to use new approaches (and got more job satisfaction, too). This also eliminated most of the need for specifications writers and people who checked to see if these rules were being followed.

One reason that the Catholic Church needs only three layers of management is that its clerics share a vision of purpose and a culture with its own strong set of values. Another is that they all understand the Church's core business processes of saving souls and administering to the needs of parishioners. Vision, culture, and understanding do more to control their actions and decisions than rules or procedures. Government and private executives would do well to learn this lesson.

How much improvement should we expect from restructuring?

This depends on the performance of your current processes and activities. If you have critical processes that operate at 50 percent non-value added now, then consider reducing this to, at most, 20 or 30 percent as you restructure. The value analysis you did to develop the 50 percent figure will show you where to find these improvements. Because the non-value added figure is so high, there should be more than just "low-hanging fruit" on the improvement tree-- you'll find plenty of windfalls on the ground.

Restructuring also presents the opportunity to reengineer processes even if they have high value added. This is especially true when information technology enables you to make significant gains in performance or service. Because the most effective reengineering projects are cross-functional, their target processes require some restructuring anyway.

Redeploying People During Restructuring

One of the great challenges to government restructuring is redeploying its human resources. All too often, organizations fail to move people out of improved or eliminated activities into new value added jobs, or simply let them go. There is no way to save money in this situation. In fact, those idle hands will find something to do that may end up costing even more money than before.

Skilled, loyal employees do not have to be dismissed, especially those in areas that will experience increased work load in the future. The 3M Corporation is a good example of this. Today, 3M has three times the amount of business as 10 years ago, but still has about the same number of people. The company did this by looking for opportunities to reduce the resources needed for some processes. Then it moved people from those processes to other processes that needed more resources to keep up with demand, or to new processes just starting up.

What 3M did was to substitute development for growth. Had it simply "grown" its work force in response to demand, the company probably would have lost market share to more effective competitors. Instead, it developed effectiveness in its processes and people. Redeployment was a key tool in doing that.

Summary

Since the early 1980s most of corporate America has been restructuring to be competitive in a turbulent world market. The end of the Cold War is causing major restructuring in the military, and new technology and fiscal austerity have just started to do the same in civilian organizations.

Will this constant change end soon? Not likely, and it may have just begun. Corporate America has learned a hard lesson about simple downsizing: not much changes except the stress levels of the survivors. Most corporations are going back to try and reduce the work they do, so that they truly can get by with fewer workers. The wisest of these companies are getting set to do continuous restructuring as they reengineer and redesign for the 21st century.

So how to you prepare for this? There are only five things to do, which are all easier when you do them routinely:

1. **Find out what customers want.** Customer expectations are the foundation for determining everything else on this list.

2. **Know what you are doing.** Map your processes and activities, know your costs, and understand what drives them.

3. **Know why you are doing it.** Routinely challenge the underlying assumptions of processes—yesterday's reasons may not be right tomorrow.

4. **Get rid of non-value added work.** Besides wasting resources, it tends to attract more non-value added work.

5. **Build in continuous improvement.** Structure processes so that they can be continually improved and check to make sure they are.

New Principles from Chapter 9

Restructuring

Old Rule or Practice	New Principle or Practice

Old Rule or Practice	New Principle or Practice

Chapter

10

Government Suppliers

- A government organization's suppliers form an integral part of the chain of processes and activities that creates value for customers. Their activities and performance affect the costs and quality of the products and services government provides.

- In many cases, government suppliers' use of activity costing and management can reduce government costs, provide better information for contracts management, and help improve cross-functional processes in which suppliers participate.

- Activity costing and management can also benefit contractors by helping them increase their competitiveness, reduce costs, and improve quality.

"Competition is a task master that protects the public. But there are penalties as well as rewards in a competitive society. . . Business must accept the penalties of failure."

—Courtney C. Brown, Columbia
University School of Business

Many government organizations have partners in providing products and services to their customers. These partners are the contractors and distributors who extend your ability to fulfill your mandate and get the job done. As Figure 10-1 illustrates, government's suppliers are an integral part of the chain of processes and activities inside and outside an organization that creates value for customers. Each member of this team affects the cost and quality of activities it supports. When process improvements are confined to inside operations, a government organization's ability to control costs and improve value also is restricted.

Figure 10-1
The Government
Value Chain

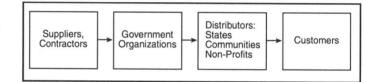

Who Are Your Partners?

A variety of product and service suppliers can be part of a government organization's value chain. The most important include:

- Service contractors, who perform tasks such as developing publications, conducting training, or running an information or computer center

- Facilities operations contractors, who manage government facilities such as laboratories and nuclear sites

- Defense and aerospace contractors, who design and build products for the military

- Municipal services contractors, who help cities and towns plow snow, collect trash and recyclables, fix pot-holes, and, increasingly, provide white-collar services such as school system management

- Other government agencies who serve as distributors in the network, such as universities that help administer Department of Education grants and loans on their campuses, or the local community health clinics that provide federal- and state-funded health care to local residents.

When partners like these follow Activity-Based Management, government, its customers, and supplier organizations themselves can benefit.

Benefits to Government and Customers of the Activity-Based Approach

All government agencies that use contractor support have a stake in contractor costs and contractor quality. Most often, government has affected contractor costs principally by seeking competitive bids and awarding contracts based on cost considerations and by conducting audits that verify a contractor's expenses and indirect costs. Although these mechanisms can save money for the government, they do not help contractors bring better cost information, reduced activity costs, or process improvements into the value chain. Using activity costing and management can achieve this, especially when both government and suppliers share this approach.

Providing more specific cost information for management and planning

Activity costing for contractors can show government managers the true costs of each aspect of contract tasks. This specific information can help set priorities for getting the most from available contract dollars. Along with the cost data on your own activities, you may find that some activities you are buying from suppliers would be cheaper to perform in-house, and vice versa. For example, if a contractor's costs for training activities were higher than the costs of similar training done by in-house staff, you might decide to train more internal trainers for future programs rather than rely on contractor support. Activity data can also show when services you buy from other government agencies cost more than those available from the private sector. You may also learn that some contractor activity costs are disproportionate compared with others, and you can decide whether they add enough value to justify their purchase.

Reducing overall costs

Activity costing can help contractors to develop more reliable cost bids, thereby reducing the risk of cost overruns and (upward) contract modifications. Activity-Based Management can also reduce overhead rates. According to the Defense Contract Audit Agency, the traditional accounting approach of using direct labor as the allocation base for indirect labor tends to increase overhead rates. In addition, the process improvements that activity management helps identify can save contractors money. Subsequent bids on government projects will usually reflect these savings as contractors try to improve their competitive position.

Improving quality and performance for customers

If your contractor can cut cycle time for printing materials and mailing services, you can get your products to customers more quickly. If your telephone hotline contractor develops common activity definitions across its regional offices, the hotline can standardize its services to customers and assess each office on common performance measures. If your contractor can improve the parts delivery process, you can better predict and meet your aircraft repair schedule.

Removing communication barriers

Activity definitions, from basic terminology to those in

activity dictionaries, create a common language for government and its contractors. These shared definitions help those on different ends of a cross-functional process to overcome communications barriers in addressing common goals and performing to specification.

An activity approach is not a panacea for creating better contract results, costs, or relationships. It might not benefit every contract situation. When a government agency simply buys goods from a supplier in the short term, for example, there may be less reason to care about the company's ability to improve its processes. If the company can't compete on cost or quality, you can choose someone else the next time. The greatest likelihood of government benefit from suppliers' using activity costing and management occurs when the government has a long-term relationship with a supplier or when a purchased item or service is key to the quality of a product or service the government provides.

Private Sector Experience

Around the world, companies in the private sector are increasingly adopting activity-based costing systems. A 1990 study conducted by a Canadian accounting organization found that 30 percent of U.S. firms were using or were considering using ABC. About 14 percent of Canadian and 33 percent of British companies had implemented a system.[22] Pete Zampino, director of Advanced Management Programs for the Consortium for Advanced Manufacturing International (CAM-I), told us he estimates that 5 to 10 percent of U.S. manufacturing firms are using Activity-Based Management; engineering, software development, and administrative companies are also beginning to get involved.

Some of America's largest and best-known firms are among the activity innovators, and their positive experiences show why. At Chrysler Corporation, for example, an ABC pilot project in 1992 focused on the cross-functional process of designing wiring harnesses for minivans. Nine departments were involved in determining how many harnesses should be used, and every group had a different point of view and a different self-interest. The group that would have to assemble the harnesses wanted only one to be used; the design department wanted nine. ABC cost information on activities across the production process clearly showed that the magic number for cost efficiency was two harnesses—avoiding the protracted squabbles that would have occurred without objective data. The pilot experience convinced Chrysler to implement ABC across the board.[23]

At General Electric Medical Systems, which services imaging machines for medical facilities, ABC data have helped the company achieve eight percent increases in productivity for two years running.[24] Westinghouse, Inc., Western Zirconium introduced ABC to help minimize overhead allocations and provide the specific financial information needed to decentralize management. The company also found that cost information increased the visibility of non-value added support department activities—and led to their elimination.[25] Crum and Forster Commercial Insurance benefits from the detail and accuracy of its ABC system in evaluating the efficiency of its operations across different regions. Managers also use the information to estimate required staffing levels, make confident product and pricing decisions, and set minimum premium amounts.[26]

One Contractor's Experience

A Department of Energy (DOE) management and operations contractor, EG&G, is an example of a government supplier that is using activity costing and management as a basis for improving processes and eliminating non-value added activities. Based on positive results at several of its 24 divisions and its corporate headquarters, the company decided to apply activity costing and management in its five DOE facilities management sites.

The first pilot project took place at DOE's Mound facility in Miamisburg, Ohio. Mound's major purpose used to be constructing timers and detonators for bombs and other components of nuclear weapons. Demand for these products dropped when the Cold War ended, and the site's biggest job today is preparing the facility for conversion to civilian use.

According to the EG&G manager who coordinates the effort, the company decided to apply activity costing and management at Mound for several reasons. "We want a better understanding of the work done at the five DOE sites. We see a need to bring some standardization to processes each site shares; right now each has its unique way of doing things. We want to create a work-driven management system, rather than a functional management style."

Mound also had an immediate, compelling need to change: the facility was given a near-term deadline to cut up to 40 percent of its work force. Managers needed a rational way to reduce work, along with labor and other budget reductions.

"Anything we learn about our processes makes us much more effective in downsizing," says the EG&G manager. "In addition, our customer is now more focused on costs, so we have to be, too. Before we changed our accounting and management control system, it was difficult to see a clear path between what was funded and what work resulted. Now we can begin to look at variances in work packages instead of departmental budgets, and that tells you a lot more about efficiency, productivity, and quality. We also can be more accurate in our cost estimates by understanding the process-activity-task relationships in our work."

Managers at Mound also see another potential benefit to the operation and to DOE: the ability to track the costs of complying with regulations. This information should be a powerful rationale at DOE for eliminating many of these non-value added activities.

Although the Mound project is too new to have produced results, outcomes of Value Cost Improvement at other EG&G sites show reason for optimism. At EG&G Rotron in Woodstock, New York, managers used a pilot project to analyze the entire overhead structure and map its 12 business processes. Activity analysis revealed that almost 50 percent of activities were non-value added and identified several million dollars in possible cost savings. Following process improvements, overhead costs are down more than 10 percent, with overall savings estimated at more than $1 million per year. Positive results like these have been the norm for other EG&G projects as well. The chief financial officer at EG&G says, "We think the savings on every project so far have far outweighed the estimated costs."[27]

Costing Issues for Government Contractors

Because the government audits all of its contractors, suppliers need to be sure their auditing agency understands and accepts the ABC system. Some defense contractors have found that audit concerns are a major barrier to adopting ABC in their environment. One concern is that in switching from a traditional accounting system to ABC, they might be in violation of cost accounting standards regulations. Such regulations are designed to promote consistency in defense contractor cost estimating, allocating, accumulating, and reporting.

Another regulation, the Truth in Negotiations Act, requires that contractors disclose to the government at the time of price agreement all the significant cost and pricing data used in developing their bids. If a contractor bids a job under a traditional accounting system and adopts ABC during the contract, the firm is obligated to give the government both sets of costs. When costs or overhead rates change under ABC, the government will continue to pay the lower of the two figures, reducing the contractor's incentive to learn about activity costs. Contractors also worry that if they lower their overhead rates based on ABC—which is likely—auditors may apply the new rate retroactively and demand a refund on products or services already delivered at the old rate.

Pete Zampino of CAM-I notes that concerns such as these have stalled wider adoption of ABC among defense contractors in his consortium. "Ultimately, I believe these issues have to be resolved because Activity-Based Management-style improvements are necessary for reinventing government and reducing the deficit. Private industry knows ABC can benefit them, too, so both sides have something to gain."

Even when defense contractors feel constrained by potential audit agency rulings, they can still pursue ABC analysis of activities as part of a process improvement effort. Value analysis and performance measures do not require financial data to be useful. Also, a stand-alone ABC information data base need not be integrated into a financial information system. Finally, there is a difference between undertaking pilot projects (see Chapter 12) and full-scale change of an accounting system.

Working With Your Partners in the Value Chain

In developing your organization's Activity-Based Management system, it will be important to map and develop information about complete cross-functional processes, including those with activities that suppliers perform. Government organizations and their contractors can help each other maximize the potential of this approach. For example, agencies can share activity definitions with their suppliers to create a common frame of reference. They can also educate contractors about activity costing and management methodology and its potential benefits and work with suppliers to overcome audit-related barriers. As government activity data suggest process improvements involving contractors, agencies can spell out the kinds of work processes suppliers need to develop.

Government organizations have also had contractors raise their awareness about Activity-Based Management. For example, based on discussions with its contractor, EG&G, the Department of Energy became interested in Activity-Based Management and is now assessing the possibility of using the approach in some of its own operations.

Every organization has been burned by low-price suppliers who turned out to be disasters. By understanding both sides of the activities of the supplier/customer cost and operations activity picture, governments will find more low-cost suppliers. A low-cost supplier is one who delivers defect-free products and services just when you need them. Today, such suppliers let you place and pay invoices electronically, which cuts your internal administrative cost. Most of all, they are the type of lean, flexible partners who put value in the value chain.

ABC and Vendor Partnerships

In the private sector many companies have decided to drastically trim the number of vendors and suppliers they use. Instead, these companies give more business to a few highly-qualified and responsible vendors who will meet their demands for high-quality goods, at low prices, delivered just in time.

In return, the vendors agree to extra requirements. These include taking part in process and product design and improvement and following some of the buyer's management practices. To date, these practices have included statistical process control and other quality management methods. Before long it should include the use of ABC as a common process and cost language.

Summary

Activity-Based Management produces the greatest results when it is applied to improve all the processes and activities in a government organization's value chain. Government organizations can raise contractors' awareness of the benefits and methods of the activity approach and work with them to create a mutually beneficial, activity-based perspective.

New Principles from Chapter 10

Government Suppliers

Old Rule or Practice	New Principle or Practice

Old Rule or Practice	New Principle or Practice

PART IV

INITIATING ACTIVITY COSTING AND MANAGEMENT

Chapter

11

Change Management

- Many attempts to introduce new management approaches fail because people do not support them.

- Government agencies make the change to activity-based costing and Activity-Based Management a productive reality by using the methodology and techniques of change management: the process of helping the people in an organization adapt to new organizational strategies, systems, processes, or structures.

- These same methods can be used to help people adjust to the improvements that result from using ABC and Activity-Based Management.

"The decision which achieves organization objectives must be both (1) technologically sound and (2) carried out by people. If we lose sight of the second requirement or if we assume naively that people can be made to carry out whatever decisions are technically sound—we run the risk of decreasing rather than increasing the effectiveness of the organization."

—Douglas McGregor,
management pioneer

In the film *Field of Dreams*, a man builds a baseball field to attract the ghosts of famous ball players. He does this upon hearing a mysterious voice saying, "If you build it, they will come." Does this work for ABC and Activity-Based Management? Here is part of an interview we conducted for this book. The government financial officer interviewed had helped introduce activity-based costing to his organization.

> *Coopers & Lybrand:* What type of ABC information do you give to managers and supervisors in the field?

> *Financial Officer* (pulling out thick book of computer printouts): We gave this cost analysis to all of them. It has detailed cost data by activity for each major process in each district.

> *C&L:* How have they used this information to improve their operations?

> *Financial Officer:* You know, they haven't used it, and I can't figure out why. It's detailed, accurate data, so it ought to be useful.

> *C&L:* Did you give them any training on how to use the information?

> *Financial Officer:* That sounds like a good idea.

This common mistake is what Robert S. Kaplan calls the "field of dreams" mentality: If we give managers and employees activity data, they will use it productively. In fact, the opposite is usually true. Unless organizations promote, enable, and reinforce the activity approach to management, it is never fully implemented; it does not lead to the actions and improvements that maximize its value.

Innovation: Something that is new to an organization. It can include technology, information systems, processes, rules, or some aspect of organizational culture. ABC is a management information innovation; Activity-Based Management in a management approach innovation.

Change: The process of introducing and sustaining an innovation.

Change sponsor: The individual or group who legitimizes and champions an innovation. For ABC and Activity-Based Management to succeed, this must be one or more members of top management.

Change agent: The individual(s) or groups(s) who develop and introduce an innovation. For ABC, often this is a team of managers, supported by internal and external specialists such as accountants and consultants.

Change target: The individual or groups who must accept and use the innovation. In ABC, these are management, employee, and sometimes supplier personnel who will make decisions based on ABC information. Change targets vary during the life of a change management project; usually, the first targets are change sponsors.

Change advocate: The individuals or groups who want to see an innovation succeed, but do not have the power or resources to make the change happen. Often, change advocates stimulate an organization to start an ABC initiative. They may include members of a board of directors, internal managers or employees, accountants, or external customers, regulatory groups, and other stakeholders in the organization.

Figure 11-1
Key Terms in Change Management

Change Management: Integral, Not Incidental

Government agencies make the change to the activity-based way a productive reality by using the methodology and techniques of change management: the process of helping the people in an organization adapt to innovations such as new organizational strategies, systems, processes, or structures. Under our change management methodology, organizations begin supporting change at the same time they begin making it. Each step of technical planning and implementation has a complementary change management component.

Figure 11-2
Factors That
Enable the
Change
to Activity-Based
Management

Elements	Outcomes
Accountability	• Determination of specific roles, goals, and performance measures for managers and employees under Activity-Based Management.
Communication	• Strategy to learn from successful and unsuccessful change actions that are taken to support Activity-Based Management.
Focus, Purpose, and Vision	• Plan to influence all those who will sponsor, support, implement or be affected by Activity-Based Management including displacement planning if necessary. • Plan for ensuring that those affected by Activity-Based Management participate fully in decisions and implementation.
Leadership	• Mission statement and guiding principle for the Activity-Based Management vision. • Specification of the results sought and criteria for evaluating progress and success.

Elements	Outcomes
Measurement	• Plan for leadership actions to be taken and infrastructure designed to promote and enable Activity-Based Management.
	• Plan for dealing with the cultural aspects of adopting Activity-Based Management based on an assessment of the organization's readiness to change.
	• Plan for the involvement of and teaming with bargaining units.
Momentum	• Determination of data to be used to track implementation.
	• Determination of the measurable improvements to be achieved by Activity-Based Management.
	• Leadership plan for responding to shifts in the pace of implementation of change actions or acceptance.
Recognition and Rewards	• Plan to reward and recognize managers and employees based on Activity-Based Management-related criteria and to provide sanctions for those who do not meet the critieria.
Skill Development	• Plan for providing training to prepare for and enable effective participation in Activity-Based Management at all levels.
Team Orientation	• Plan to use teams throughout the organization to manage, implement and take ownership of Activity-Based Management.

Figure 11-2 (cont.)
Factors That
Enable the
Change
to Activity-Based
Management

Because each agency's culture, structure, and personnel are unique, one size does not fit all in managing change. The key factors that enable successful change listed in Figure 11-2 must be tailored to each agency's needs and situation. By addressing these factors during the Assess and Plan stages of change management, agencies can create their own individual "change maps" to guide and coordinate leadership actions throughout the process. This plan for managing the change works side-by-side with the plan for adopting Activity-Based Management.

Most successful change scenarios include these four characteristics:

1. **Compelling need.** The need for ABC information and process improvement is real and urgent. Making this change may even be a matter of survival. People in the organization understand and accept the need for change.

2. **Overcoming barriers.** The organization anticipates resistance to Activity-Based Management and views it as a positive sign of engagement in the issue. Leaders also plan and carry out ways to overcome resistance and other barriers to adopting Activity-Based Management.

3. **Change management roles.** People in the organization have, accept, and understand defined roles in the change process that they play effectively. Leadership is committed to the adoption and use of Activity-Based Management.

4. **Providing support.** Change sponsors provide the systems, human resources, and other organizational supports needed to make change happen. They also recognize that major change traumatizes an organization and that the ability to absorb and respond to change is finite. The organization regularly takes its own pulse and helps the work force stay motivated, keep pace, and sustain ABC and Activity-Based Management.

Such integration of the technical and behavioral aspects of change ensures that neither element is overshadowed by the other. It also helps organizations maintain the focus on the desired outcomes of the change to Activity-Based Management—not simply on the tasks and steps required along the way.

Compelling Need

Keeping quiet about ABC can doom it to failure, as one manufacturing company learned the hard way. One accountant designed the ABC system virtually in secret, under direct orders not to communicate about the effort until the system was ready for use. Top management considered Activity-Based Management to be "a petty accounting detail" and didn't want to hear about it before, during, or after its development. Other key staff were angry and fearful when the announcement was made and began bickering among themselves about its impact. No further communication occurred—and no one in the company ever learned to use the valuable information the system could have provided.[28]

In any technical project, you begin by identifying and defining a problem that must be solved or an opportunity to be gained, and the solution or innovation that will address it. In change management, the *need* to address the problem or opportunity becomes the "compelling reason" for change that must be communicated to everyone.

"Selling" the compelling reason to your people is one of the most critical challenges of change management. If they understand why you must introduce activity costing and management, and if the reason appears important to them, those who will be affected by this innovation will be more likely to support it. This is true even if there may be negative consequences for some individuals and groups.

Here are some examples of compelling needs that drove many organizations mentioned in this book to adopt activity costing and management:

- Deep budget cuts and major Navy fleet reductions caused many Naval shipyards to drastically reduce their work forces at the end of the Cold War.

- EG&G Mound Technologies lost whole areas of its business when the end of the Cold War eliminated the need for many of its products.

- The U.S. Postal Service must control costs and improve service, or face a disastrous future.

- Middle managers at the Internal Revenue Service were having funding shortfalls, but they didn't know why.

- The Indianapolis Department of Public Works had to start competing for business with the private sector, but officials didn't know how much it cost to fill a pothole or pick up a ton of trash.

- The Phoenix, Arizona city council required that user fees finance 100 percent of the resources needed to issue permits, so that many fee-supported offices had to find ways to cut costs or justify fee increases.

Ironically, these examples indicate that the more trouble your organization is in, the more you can expect people to rally around an innovation. But do you have to be on the brink of disaster before people will accept ABC or Activity-Based Management? Not if you understand about "pain" and communication. Let's start with pain.

Most managers probably know that traditional accounting systems deliver the wrong information too late. They have to "game" those systems every day and often fight them to introduce innovations of their own. To them, such systems are pains in the neck. Employees who have been asked to control and improve their activities often lack the performance data to do so. To them, this lack is a pain.

The more "pain" people feel with the status quo, the more likely they are to accept a reasonable remedy for the pain. A sharp pain, such as a sudden budget cut, is like appendicitis: everyone knows it's there and wants to do something about it. Unfortunately, many of the management ills that activity costing and management cure are more like cancer: people do not realize they have it until too late. In that case, you must plan a careful communication campaign to educate people on the need to take the ABC cure.

Communicating about an innovation

Simply stating a compelling reason or talking about pain will raise more questions than it answers. People need to know what the future will be like with ABC and Activity-Based Management and to understand how these innovations will affect them and their work. This requires early and frequent communication throughout the course of changing.

A vision of the new way. Top management addresses these critical issues by developing and communicating a vision for change. This vision tells your organization:

- Why you need ABC or Activity-Based Management to accomplish your mission and satisfy your customers

- The benefits that will come from introducing this innovation

- How this will change the way you work

- Who will need to change (the change targets), and in what ways

- What specific customer and organizational goals these innovations will help you reach

- The milestones and time frame for introducing the innovations

- How the innovations will affect job security.

In developing a vision for change, it's important to identify your change targets, or all those who will be affected by the change, and make sure their specific concerns are addressed. At one government facility, for example, the decision to compete with private companies to provide services created a compelling need to understand and control costs. Under the new vision, when support departments didn't provide value for cost, production units could go outside for many of the services they needed. These departments required special attention in making the transition to ABC, which was part of the innovation of competition.

Job security is a particularly important issue for leaders to cover in their vision for change. Managers and employees are often frightened when they learn that the activity approach involves mapping their activities and their processes, attaching costs to them, and performing value added analysis. "What will happen to me?" is the first and most important question people ask. Without good answers, even the initial activity mapping task of ABC can be in jeopardy. A manager at a Naval shipyard, for example, recalls that when personnel heard about a layoff of nearly 25 percent, "We didn't want to hear about ABC. We wanted to know what was going to happen to us."

Managers, employees, customers, and suppliers all should learn the vision for change early in the planning process. Such openness helps avoid rumors, lack of trust, and the perception of unequal access to information (and unequal power to prosper in the new environment).

Communicating: how and when. Every organization has many ways to communicate about an innovation. Some, like the corporate newsletter and memos, are official. Others are less so, such as discussing the change with opinion leaders and managers. Use whichever communication channels are appropriate—but use them often. That way, you are sure to reach everyone with the exact message you want, and the repetition will say "This is important."

Invite response to the vision and other communications. Throughout the change process, all questions, comments, and suggestions are valuable. To show this, get back to people within 24 hours after they contact you, even if it is only to say that you appreciate their question or suggestion and are working on it. You will win people over with such respect for their opinions, even if they are ambivalent or initially negative about ABC or Activity-Based Management.

Overcoming Barriers

Barriers are technical and social, formal and informal road blocks that prevent or inhibit change targets from adopting desired behaviors.

Technical barriers

The following often are "Catch 22s" of introducing ABC:

- Requirements that all decisions to change costs or invest in process improvement be made using traditional accounting methods. Don't laugh about this. Even during ABC implementation, some organizations neglect to spread the word that it is an acceptable input for such decisions.

- Absence of information systems that would convey ABC data to managers and employees to use in process improvement.

- As noted in Chapter 9, some organizations discovered to their dismay that external auditors who did not understand or accept ABC could potentially cause major problems in the area of allowable costs. This halted their ABC initiatives.

The first of these technical barriers can be removed by executive order or by the design of the ABC system. The second barrier requires the design and introduction of a process-oriented improvement system, something that has to be done before or along with introducing ABC as an input to improvement. The last is a legal and policy problem that must be overcome before you start to introduce ABC.

Behavioral barriers

Management style and organizational culture. Does the existing management style lend itself to using ABC tools and techniques? For example:

- Managers' "gut feelings" may take precedence over objective information, meaning ABC data will be ignored. On the other hand, your organization may strongly value objective decision-making, which will be a plus for ABC.

- Your organization has a culture of blame that punishes individuals for process problems they cannot control, or "shoots the messenger" who reports a problem. Conversely, your culture may view problems as opportunities, and reward people for identifying them.

If you happen to have a culture of blame, then prepare for an unparalleled level of fear and resistance. That's because ABC discovers so many problems. To succeed, it must become known as "amnesty-based costing"—there is no punishment associated with its initial findings.

Resistance. Said one Postal Service manager, "ABC may be the best thing since sliced bread, but if all you've ever had is sliced bread, you resist it." Often, managers may resist the idea that any such technique can help them make better decisions, saying things like:

"We don't even use the old system—we have to operate around it to get things done around here."
"What do accountants know about running my operation?"
"So someone's going to come in and dissect my job and measure my performance by their new standards. Sounds like another way to blame me for problems I can't control."

You would expect more sympathy from accountants, but often they are the most resistant to change. Many see no problem with existing cost systems. Many prefer to crunch numbers instead of interacting with people. ABC forces accountants and line managers to work together, and the former may not be comfortable with such interaction. Most of all, cost systems are accountants' turf, and they will resist others who trespass on it. Attempts by nonaccountants to reform that system may be viewed as personal or professional criticism, and possibly even as a career threat. Bringing your accountants on board the team that develops ABC is thus very important.

Fear. Fear can be a major cause of resistance to change, one that you need to diagnose and deal with whenever it occurs. To do this, you will find it useful to distinguish between two types of fear about change:

- **Fear of new things.** Most people are at least somewhat afraid to try new ways of doing things. Part of this may be due to a fear of failure, and another part may be a simple aversion to anything unknown. Both of these causes have the same root: a fear of losing control of one's life.

  Such fears are relatively easy to alleviate. For example, through education and communication you can clarify what ABC is, how it will be used, and the role individuals have in using it. Training that allows people to experiment with using ABC lowers the stress associated with fear of failure. Using pilot or demonstration projects permits people to observe ABC and its results, which may satisfy their need to know about the future.

- **Fear of loss.** This can include loss of job, prestige, salary, and control. To the extent that ABC enables a better sharing of authority and accountability among all personnel, those who may see themselves losing power may fear it.

Some people's fear of loss is justified: they may lose power, autonomy, or even their jobs as a result of ABC. For example, in some cases ABC tools and techniques are used to determine who will be affected by a downsizing, so when they hear ABC, some people think of layoffs. In other cases, the fear has no basis in fact: ABC does not threaten the role of accountants (it can in fact expand that role).

Whether a fear about ABC has a real or imagined basis, you are wise to treat the *perception* of the fear as a reality to change targets. This is best done through open, active communication about ABC, its operation, and its intended results. This is why our approach to change management emphasizes continued communication: it dispels imaginary fears with facts. This even enables people with real fears to regain control of their lives because now they know what the future will bring and can plan accordingly.

Overcoming resistance

At one government organization, initial resistance to ABC took the form of inaction; people got the ABC data, but they did nothing with it. At another organization, resistance was both active and covert: workers figured out how to manipulate the system to appear responsive while continuing business as usual.

Two strategies can help organizations avoid destructive results like these and use resistance constructively. First, it is important to assess potential resistance early in planning. When concerns are known, the vision and plans for change can openly address and deal with "human factor" problems before they occur. Tools such as cultural surveys can provide objective information about the most important human concerns. Structured interviews with individuals and groups, as well as informal feedback mechanisms, can also provide baseline information about people's readiness for change.

Second, people resist change more strongly when it is simply imposed upon them. Involving those affected by ABC and Activity-Based Management in determining how the new system will be used and how their jobs will change helps build commitment from the outset. Working cooperatively with both individuals and employee bargaining units is important. For example, the mayor of Indianapolis won over the public employees' union by involving its leadership in ABC-related decisions. He paid attention to union concerns such as offering alternative jobs and retraining to union employees whose jobs were affected by cost efficiencies. The union's executive director says that they've come around because the relationship between the mayor and the union "is substantive and real. A lot of the recommendations we make, he's taken to heart."[29]

When organizations recognize resistance and uncover its root causes, they can take action to overcome it. Besides frequent communications, effective approaches include:

Scheduling speedy pilot projects to produce early positive results. Nothing overcomes skepticism like hard data on positive results. Cooper and Kaplan reported on managers' responses to the results of two ABC pilot projects at a water technology company. Managers' comments on seeing the results included: "I ... was sold right away. Now I know where the costs are." "It can be used right away to support our day-to-day discount decisions." "In retrospect, I wish that my people had been more involved in the process ... I wasn't sure what ABC was about ... Next time, I'd dedicate at least one of my people to the project."[30] Chapter 12 provides more details on using pilot projects.

Demonstrating the organization's commitment to long-term use. Providing visible management support and organizational supports, as discussed in the next section, shows resisters that the activity way is here to stay—and they might as well get on board.

Roles in the Change Process

As Figure 11-1 shows, people in an organization play four key roles during the adoption of ABC and Activity-Based Management. Although only a few are change sponsors, change agents, and change advocates, everyone who needs to use or understand the new system is a change target. In fact, change sponsors and agents are all change targets before they become innovation supporters. Converting them to the new way is the job of change advocates and other change sponsors and agents.

What happens when these roles are not played the right way? Two examples of disaster show the importance of assigning change management roles wisely. They occurred at neighboring government facilities, each of which developed ABC systems with poor results.

At one, the change sponsor was interested in ABC but only marginally committed to its success and "too busy" to have hands-on involvement. He delegated leadership to change agents who didn't have the support or authority to make change happen. He also retired as soon as the ABC system was introduced, leaving no sustaining sponsors to take his place. Although excellent people helped develop the system and change targets knew how to apply it, ABC has rarely been used at the facility for decision-making or improvement.

At the facility next door, the change sponsor was effective, committed, stayed with the project, and made many of the right moves. The people assigned to develop and implement ABC and to act as change agents, however, were those who "had time" or "needed coverage," not necessarily the most competent staff. Equally bad, they did not come from among the change targets most relevant for institutionalizing the approach. In addition to compromising development of the system, these assignments sent a clear signal to other change targets that ABC was not a serious organizational priority—and this facility had the same null outcome as its neighbor.

Understanding the roles

The success of change depends on all change management roles being known and understood by each player and leadership roles being assigned to the right people and played effectively. Based on eight case studies on introducing ABC to private companies, failure is most likely to occur when:

- The initial change sponsor fails to identify sustaining change sponsors for the project's implementation phase, when people must begin to use the information to make improvements, or

- The change sponsor fails to identify the targets of change, with the result that the people who ultimately must use ABC information are not involved early enough in the process to buy into the change. They also don't learn to understand and use the system as it's being developed, guaranteeing at best a lag time between implementation and application.[31]

Change sponsors. At the IRS, the change sponsor is the organization's Chief Financial Officer (CFO). From the start, he recognized the need to involve other change sponsors to sustain and institutionalize the approach. Says a manager who works for the CFO: "He's looking for and finding support among the field directors, and the effort is getting good reception in the field. If he leaves, it will go on, because 10 to 15 key executives he's helped bring on board would make sure that it doesn't die."

As we discuss in Chapter 12, usually the CEO or other top executives must become the change sponsor for ABC or Activity-Based Management. This is because both innovations are fundamental, organization-wide change. Regardless of who is chosen, effective sponsorship is critical and, in our experience, no major change can succeed without it. Figure 11-3 lists some of the characteristics strong sponsors need to develop.

Figure 11-3
Characteristics of
an Effective
Change Sponsor

Characteristic	Definition
Power	The organizational power to legitimize Activity-Based Management with the targets.
Pain	A personal stake in making Activity-Based Management succeed to the extent that the current situation is more painful/costly than the change.
Vision	A total, in-depth understanding of what change must occur to implement Activity-Based Management, and the effect the change will have on the organization.
Public Role	The willingness and ability to demonstrate commitment to, and active public support for, Activity-Based Management.
Private Role	The willingness and ability to meet privately with agents to discuss progress, problems, and concerns with the change effort.
Performance Management	The willingness and ability to reward desired behaviors and confront undesirable behaviors in regard Activity-Based Management.
Sacrifice	The commitment to pursue Activity-Based Management despite the personal or political prices that may be paid.

Change agents are also important to success. They lead the teams that develop ABC systems and projects, and they are often managers or key leaders of units that will use the information produced. Change agents need to understand the processes about which activity information is gathered and the cultural aspects of how work gets done. They help staff understand the benefits of an innovation, work to overcome resistance, and learn how to use the system.

Change advocates. More than just a "cheering section" for change, these advocates support innovation by making their interests known to top management. Outside change advocates, such as the National Performance Review and the federal Office of Management and Budget, develop convincing reasons for change. Inside advocates, such as line managers who want better cost information, get the message across in meetings with executives. These managers are also first in line to try new approaches they support.

When the system is in place, change sponsors and change agents model the behaviors appropriate to ABC and Activity-Based Management. Just by referring to activity information, asking questions about it, or factoring it into their decisions, they get others to pay attention to it. Nothing sends a stronger message that the change is real than managers' walking the walk as well as talking the talk.

Choosing the best and brightest

Who are the right people to lead Activity-Based Management change management? Every organization will have its own answer to that question. Experience suggests that when financial officers take the lead, operating managers must also play key roles to avoid isolating ABC as an "accounting project." Ideally, all those involved in leading and implementing the activity way will be the bright, capable, respected people organizations value most—at all levels of responsibility. They should also be people who are expected to remain part of the organization for the foreseeable future.

Developing Organizational Supports

Developing organizational systems and human resources policies and programs to support the adoption of Activity-Based Management is a critical aspect of managing change. Figure 11-4 shows the elements in an organization that drive behavior; the more these elements are constructed to support ABC and Activity-Based Management, the greater the ability to drive behavior in the desired directions.

Figure 11-4
Organizational
Supports

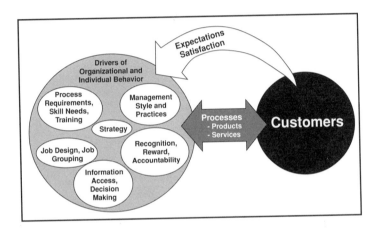

Training

For example, managers and employees can't be expected to use ABC if they don't understand the system and have the attitudes and skills to use it. *Training* is often required to help people create and use activity information effectively. At one Naval shipyard, ABC was initially perceived as a top-down program; people got the data the system produced, but they didn't use it. Training, which included TQM-style sessions designed to develop leadership skills, a customer focus, and a continuous improvement mentality, complemented specific ABC how-to information and tools. This training enabled people to accept and work with the new system.

Training may also be needed to help managers develop the skills and attitudes they need to change their management style and pay more attention to activity costs. Such training may include discussion of new organizational values that give managers the authority and flexibility to use activity information to make changes. Managers often need permission to change their styles, notes an IRS section chief. "You have to challenge people to make the system more sensible, but you can't hurt the risk-takers; you can't kill people for trying."

Information access

Another requisite for ABC success is an information system (IS) that provides timely Activity-Based Management data in a user-friendly format to all those who can use it. Management must make the commitment to provide proper information support, and involve information systems representatives in the change management process. At one large government organization, for example, IS personnel were brought into Activity-Based Management development after many significant decisions affecting them had already been made. Their predictable resistance was a major barrier to implementing the process.

The Examinations Division of the Boston IRS District developed both a useful information system and an approach to promoting its use. The system was designed to produce quarterly data that plotted trends on key measures. Branch managers were instructed to explain the results each time reports came in. Activity performance measures were added to the annual management by objective goals for branch and group managers. Also, managers were informed of specific types of decisions in which they were expected to consider activity information.[32]

Rewards and recognition

By adding activity performance measures to the management by objective goals, the Boston District also addressed another key driver of change, *recognition, reward, and performance management*. Two types of actions can affect this driver: providing incentives to use Activity-Based Management and making people accountable for cost outcomes.

Key *incentives*, of course, relate to the performance management system—rewarding desired behaviors with good evaluations, raises, and promotions. Managers and employees can also be appreciated informally with praise or symbolic recognition such as certificates, plaques, and ceremonies. IRS headquarters created a group incentive to use Activity-Based Management information to save money by agreeing to give a portion of the savings back to the local division. At the Hartford office, field agents started looking at the data to see where reducible costs lay. In one instance, they started using less expensive gasoline for their cars when they saw the impact of that cost component.

Accountability

Accountability is the other side of the performance management coin. The mayor of Indianapolis made whole departments accountable for their costs by making them compete with private sector groups for city contracts. Individual accountability begins with performance goals and evaluation criteria that emphasize desired behaviors.

Organizational supports are the nuts and bolts of change management. Although leadership and communication are critical, these practical steps are the building blocks of change.

Managing the Outcomes of Success

As they come on line, ABC and Activity-Based Management create many changes in an organization. This is good, healthy innovation that will improve operations and deliver better results to customers—but it can still cause human problems. Fortunately, you can apply the same change management techniques that support the adoption of ABC and Activity-Based Management to the subsequent changes they produce.

The most difficult issue concerns people who lose their positions due to improvements. These create three special change management needs:

- Supporting managers through the process of dealing with civil service regulations and employee bargaining units to make needed cuts.

- Helping employees who must leave to cope with their situation through offering job counseling or outplacement services, providing retraining for employment in other divisions or agencies, and creating consulting agreements with former employees for valuable, but occasional, services.

- Helping employees who remain cope with their sense of loss, guilt, and resentment about the changes. Good communication is critical for organizations to work through these periods constructively. Just as essential is making the commitment to streamline work processes as you streamline staff. Otherwise, the change will only mean that those who remain must cope with their jobs plus the jobs of those who left.

Some compare managing organizational change to keeping all the parts of a mobile in balance.[33] Although Activity-Based Management and resulting improvement efforts may temporarily upset that balance, developing the capacity to manage the changes gives government organizations more than a short-term benefit. Change management is a valuable long-term competence that allows agencies to respond flexibly to changing customer demands and the ongoing need for continuous improvement. Organizations with a mandate to reinvent themselves cannot succeed without it.

Summary

Change management is not a nice "extra" that organizations on a budget or in a hurry can do without. It is essential to developing and using ABC and Activity-Based Management. Without change management support, introducing these innovations usually stalls—or becomes just another system people ignore or comply with rather than use.

Learning to manage organizational changes such as those surrounding Activity-Based Management is a critical skill for today's government agency. It is a core competency for all improvement-driven organizations.

New Principles from Chapter 11

Change Management

Old Rule or Practice	New Principle or Practice

Old Rule or Practice	New Principle or Practice

Chapter
12

Getting Results from Activity-Based Management

- Preparing for Activity-Based Management starts with gaining executive support and commitment. Scoping initial projects depends less on technical factors than on their strategic intent.

- Part of this intent should be to lay the groundwork for continued use of ABC or Activity-Based Management. Otherwise, first projects will be one-time efforts with limited results.

- Technical competence is critical to the credibility of early projects. Extra planning, training, and technical assistance from experienced specialists ensure this competence.

- No first project should aim at only providing information. The goal should be results measured in process improvement, cost savings, and better service to customers.

- Once Activity-Based Management is in place, it must be sustained with executive support, continued adjustments, and enhancements.

"In a Little League baseball game, a boy got a hit, ran to first base, on to second, then hesitated and yelled, 'Where is third base?' During his confusion, the shortstop put him out. We have to have a plan to take us all the way to home plate or we will get lost along the way."

—Joe Griffith,
business speaker and writer

Just what is home plate in Activity-Based Management? It's not to introduce this management innovation, or even to get people to follow its principles. It's not even getting results from your first few projects. You reach home plate when you have established systems that ensure continued results: ever-improving operations, customers and employees who become happier and more loyal every year, staying competitive—whatever your organization needs to meet its mission now and in the future. This chapter is about ensuring that you make it all the way to home plate and continue to score for the rest of the game.

Gaining Support and Setting Direction

For any fundamental change in management, reaching first base always means converting top leaders and gaining their support. Thus, your most important task in introducing Activity-Based Management is to get executives to "walk the walk" of the activity approach to business. This means they start using ABC in making their own decisions, discuss ABC information with their subordinates, and otherwise make ABC a regular part of operations. Also, executives must learn to view the organization's operations as processes, instead of simply as functions and departments.

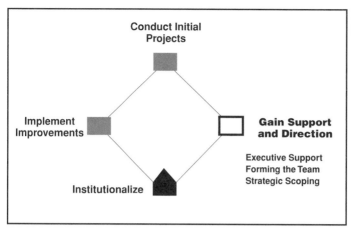

Figure 12-1
Initiating Activity-
Based
Management

Executive support

First, you have to be allowed to come to bat. Unless some
executives and top managers support ABC or Activity-
Based Management at the very start, chances are the effort
will not get underway, and if it does, it will be doomed.
Executives certainly can derail the effort by actively oppos-
ing it. Even if they seem to go along, you may not discover
some executives' opposition, or simple lack of interest, until
you are well into the initiative. When they ignore or refuse
to believe the results of activity analysis, so will their managers and employees.

As discussed in the last chapter, your first change targets
will be one or more potential change sponsors. You must
also try to win over as many other executives and senior
managers as possible and receive at least a moderate
endorsement from the rest.

This begins by educating executives about how ABC and
Activity-Based Management will benefit the organization.
Some methods for this include:

Executive briefings and seminars. Invite an outside specialist to speak on ABC and Activity-Based Management. This
can be a manager or executive from an organization that has
successfully applied these approaches, or a consultant who

specializes in it. You can ask some executives to attend outside seminars on ABC, especially those sponsored by professional associations.

Off-site visits. You can often persuade an organization that uses activity approaches to invite your executives for an on-site visit where they can discuss ABC and Activity-Based Management with their peers and other managers.

Literature and videotapes. There are many excellent articles, books, case studies, and videos about ABC and Activity-Based Management. Look for material that relates to your organization's mission or to the functional areas of individual executives. Circulate this material with an attached note explaining its importance and relevance. (It helps if the note comes from your CEO.)

Demonstrations. With a little help, in a few days you can use ABC tools and techniques to develop an internal case study of a simple process, product, or service. The results can be compared with information from the existing cost system, budget, or other data that are the accepted sources for making management decisions. Much smaller and simpler than the pilot projects discussed later in this chapter, these demonstrations can still present the dramatic differences between what your organization believes and the realities of ABC.

Individual briefings. Your first change sponsor should meet personally with every other executive and key manager in your organization to brief them on the compelling need for and benefits of the activity approach. The sponsor should explain plans for introducing it and be sure to ask for help and advice. Advice is always good, and few things commit a person more than actively helping to make change happen.

This sales job is not a one-time thing. According to a U.S. Postal Service manager, "Part way through the process, you have to go back and remind everyone where the organization is going, what the results will be, and why this will benefit them. And you have to go back and do it again and again because, in the press of daily business, people forget." Throughout the change process, you must take special pains to update executives on progress, and continue to ask them for advice and assistance. This will add momentum to executive acceptance; at the least, it will alert you to potential problems.

Forming the team

There are two key teams in a comprehensive initiative to introduce Activity-Based Management: the executive committee (top leaders) and the change team (senior and middle managers).

The executive committee. This is an optional group if you are planning limited use of ABC information, such as for a few cost studies. The executive committee is critical, though, if you intend to make ABC an integral tool for performance measurement and improvement, and it is absolutely essential for introducing Activity-Based Management.

Involving executives in creating the new approach promotes acceptance of new decision-making methods among them. If they accept and practice the new methods, so will their subordinates. Executive participation at the beginning helps to ensure that Activity-Based Management will have strong top-down guidance later.

Such a committee ideally is a small group of executives and senior managers whose operations will be affected by ABC or Activity-Based Management. The committee's job is to:

- Set policy and provide administrative guidance for both the technical and change management aspects of introducing and sustaining ABC or Activity-Based Management

- Establish and communicate the vision of the new approach to other executives, managers, employees, and suppliers

- Participate in planning sessions in their areas of expertise (e.g., the Chief Financial Officer [CFO] in costing systems discussions, the human resources chief in reward and compensation planning, etc.)

- Review and approve all implementation plans, budgets, and schedules

- Monitor progress in implementation.

Even more important, members of this committee must become role models for using ABC information in decision-making.

The change team. To implement Activity-Based Management, you will need a team made up of the executive champion, change agents, and technical and support personnel. Their responsibilities and lines of reporting should be spelled out in advance so that everyone understands their roles.

Often the chair of the steering committee, the executive champion is the sparkplug and leader of the activity initiative. He or she should be a senior executive who is well respected by peers and subordinates. This is usually not a job for the controller or CFO. Instead, select someone involved in your most important line processes, to underscore that this is more than just another accounting initiative.

Sponsors champion a change, but change agents take care of the details. They are the key contact between the change sponsor and the change targets. Change agents are responsible for such tasks as:

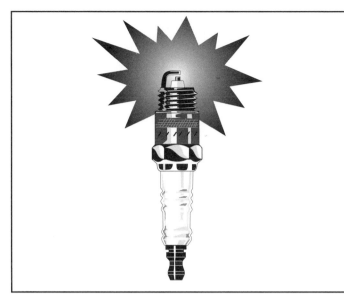

Figure 12-2
The Champion

The champion is the sparkplug and leader of the activity
initiative.

- Working with technical staff to identify the human and
  organizational aspects of the transition to Activity-Based
  Management

- Identifying problems and opportunities

- Conducting individual and focus group interviews

- Developing communication strategies and tactics

- Meeting with change targets to discuss their concerns
  about the new way

- Planning, scheduling, and monitoring the change initiative

- Facilitating planning and implementation teams made
  up of accountants, line managers, and technicians

- Discussing Activity-Based Management with key managers and employees

- Being an advocate for the interests and concerns of change targets to other managers and the change sponsor

- Planning and conducting awareness sessions on the innovations

- Giving technical assistance to change targets in activity methods and process improvement.

In most individual ABC projects like those discussed in Chapter 7, middle managers assume the role of change agent because they have much in common with the primary change targets, who are other middle and first-line managers. In introducing Activity-Based Management as a new way of doing business, executives and senior managers must initially assume change agent roles because their primary change targets are other senior leaders. Once senior leaders are on board the initiative, middle managers can begin to be used as change agents for the rest of the organization.

On both the senior and middle management levels, this similarity fosters communication, credibility, and trust between change agent and change target. To obtain this for all change targets, you may need several change agents: a line manager for other line managers, an accountant for accountants, and so on.

Finance and accounting managers and professionals can provide valuable assistance and insights on the financial aspects of ABC. Making them a key part of an Activity-Based Management initiative helps win their support for new methods of financial analysis and planning.

Information systems specialists should be on the team if you plan to integrate ABC into financial and management information systems. Having *human resource department specialists* on the team is important if you anticipate major changes in job descriptions, work force size, and other such personnel actions.

Strategic scoping

There are two levels of scoping for an Activity-Based Management initiative: tactical and strategic. Tactical scoping focuses on developing individual ABC projects and information systems, which we discussed in Chapter 7. Here we will discuss strategic scoping, the long-term view of how activity costing and management will integrate into your operations.

Strategic intent. Remember the boy who got lost on the way to third base? There should be nothing vague about the intent of your plans for Activity-Based Management. As discussed in Chapter 11, this strategic intent should be part of your vision statement for the organization after the innovations are up and running. Conducting a cost study is a tactical intent; changing costs as a result of the study is a tactical intent; providing more cost-effective services that customers value more than before is a strategic intent.

Defining strategic intent in that last way should prompt you to ask:

- Do we know what customers value? How satisfied are they now? What dissatisfies them now?

- What do we mean by "cost-effective?"

- Who and what are involved in becoming more cost-effective?

- What does it mean to manage by process and activity, instead of by function or department?

Other questions that are important to answer are listed in Appendix B. You may not know all the answers right now, but finding them in the course of early ABC or Activity-Based Management initiatives should be an objective. They show the path to home plate.

Tie in with other improvement efforts. It is not at all unusual for an organization to have several management improvement efforts going on at once. In government, these typically include quality management, time-based management, and business process reengineering (BPR), as discussed in Chapter 3. You do not want Activity-Based Management to become simply one more project, uncoordinated with the others. It is better to tie it in to existing management approaches from the very beginning.

Activity-Based Management should be an umbrella over all such individual improvement initiatives, because all are process-based management approaches and as such have a common conceptual foundation and language. ABC adds the cost and process performance information that is so often lacking in these other approaches. Finally, *managing by activity* is what all these approaches aim for; Activity-Based Management provides the structure for doing this.

Figure 12-3
Activity-Based
Management:
An Umbrella for
Other
Management
Approaches and
Methods

Activity-Based Management

Quality Management
CycleTime Reduction
Competition
Reengineering
Budgeting
Restructuring

Cost Accounting
Cost Management
Contracting
Measurement
Gainsharing
Performance Measurement
Internal Controls

Whether you use Activity-Based Management as your principal approach to management or incorporate it in another approach, involving people from other improvement initiatives is important. This helps overcome resistance to what may be perceived as a threat to their work philosophies and helps ensure that they will use ABC information. You can use their help.

For example, the manager in charge of ABC at EG&G Mound told us, "We have about 40 quality management facilitators whose job is to train and coach improvement teams. Initially, we did not include them in planning our initiative, a mistake they quickly let us know. They are key to guiding people in how to use activity data for process improvement, so we need to make sure they understand why and how we collected and analyzed the data. Their skills as facilitators are valuable to conducting our storyboarding sessions, so we made a special effort to go back and include them part way through."

Conducting Initial Projects

After all that preparation, you are ready to take a swing at the ball. Then you have to make it to first base. This is the technical work of conducting your first few ABC projects.

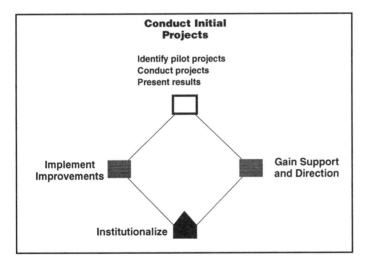

Figure 12-4
Conducting Initial
Projects

In Chapter 7, we showed you how to do this with early assessment projects, internal controls, and information systems. Here we will discuss the nature of pilot projects for introducing ABC and Activity-Based Management.

Pilot projects. Few organizations introduce ABC or Activity-Based Management at once to all parts of their operations.

Instead, they conduct a pilot project in a single large process, business unit, or work site and later expand to other areas.

There are good reasons for this. First, you need to customize activity methods to the particular needs of your organization. Second, you want to develop the internal capability to introduce these innovations, which saves money on outside consultants' fees. Third, you want to build support for the new way so that its results will be used throughout your organization. You can best accomplish these objectives by piloting or prototyping activity methods in a relatively small, manageable area.

Some organizations choose to assess one major *cross-functional process* before committing to using Activity-Based Management in other areas. The Defense Mapping Agency did its first ABC analysis on its large acquisition procurement process. A procurement process is very visible and can cause much difficulty for other processes that depend on it. Assessing procurement is thus good for calling attention to the benefits of Activity-Based Management. Another advantage is that the assessment is sure to point out how actions in other departments can bog down procurement operations, and vice versa—a good argument for more cross-functional cooperation.

The Navy shipyards and EG&G conducted activity mapping and costing and value analyses of nearly all activities in *one work site* before introducing ABC to other sites. This enabled them to develop a customized activity dictionary that could be used at all sites. As a result, both headquarters have comparable data from their field facilities. When EG&G started its assessment, the company assigned people from four other sites to observe and train at the initial Mound Nuclear site in Ohio. This gave EG&G a cadre of internal trainers, facilitators, and consultants to use at the other sites.

The Internal Revenue Service, which has hundreds of offices throughout the United States and overseas, has a five-year plan for introducing Activity-Based Management to the entire organization. This started with several *sequential pilot projects at various sites*. Analysts from headquarters and field offices conduct the assessments, focusing them on a single large process. Over the next few years the IRS will cover all its sites and processes in this manner. In the meantime its pilot projects are building local support for and capability to carry out Activity-Based Management principles and methods.

Implementing Improvements

You reach third base when you gain the first measurable improvements from using Activity-Based Management. To get the best results, you need to do the following.

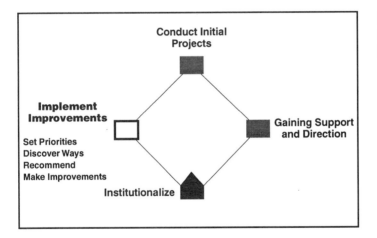

Figure 12-5
Conducting Initial
Projects

Set priorities

Using the analyses and data you have already developed, start stratifying processes, ranking them from high to low according to different attributes or other variables. For example:

- **Cost.** If your prime objective is to lower costs, find out which processes cost the most. These are your first targets.

- **Non-value added content.** Rank all the processes in a core business process by the percentage of resources consumed by non-value added activities.

- **High cost-of-quality.** Rank processes by their total percentage of poor quality costs (prevention, appraisal, internal failure, external failure).

- **Cycle time consumed.** If you are interested in speeding up operations, look for activities that consume the most time in a process.

You may also want to rank customers or groups of customers by the cost of serving them. This type of analysis is important when:

- You charge *user or permit fees* and want to adjust them to recover 100 percent of costs.

- You are supported by a *revolving or operating fund* and bill other government customers for products or services you deliver.

- You have experienced, or can expect, *changes in customer demographics or other characteristics*, which will make it more costly to meet your mission.

Discover ways to improve

This involves using ABC and other process improvement analyses and problem-solving methods to identify root causes of problems. Once the root causes are known, you can develop improvements that permanently solve the problems and increase performance.

For reasons discussed in Chapter 11, we favor involving people in developing improvements for their own activities and processes. This is especially important for major changes such as reengineering and restructuring.

Now is the time to train the individuals and teams working on improvements to use activity costing and management tools and techniques. This includes more detailed activity mapping, cost modeling, and value analysis. Use activity methods to discover appropriate performance measures for improved processes, and incorporate these measures into your recommendations.

Make recommendations

Use activity costing and management information to present improvement recommendations, performance baselines, and expected costs and benefits of improvements. With activity mapping you will also be able to show how processes will be changed and who will be involved.

Spend as much or even more time preparing improvement recommendations for management as you did for your presentation of an initial activity assessment. It will help tremendously if your formal presentation really is just a formality because you have already briefed each key decision-maker individually and gained his or her support.

Make improvements

Early success is critical in gaining acceptance for Activity-Based Management, yet, many sound recommendations for improvement, which everyone agrees with and supports, are never implemented as planned or in full. Some never make it past the drawing board. Here's what you can do to prevent this:

- **Low-hanging fruit.** Some of your initial recommendations for process improvements should be aimed at easy targets, the "low-hanging fruit" that can be harvested with little effort. This produces quick, visible results.

- **Accountability.** Someone must be accountable for every accepted recommendation. Furthermore, such improvement projects need plans, schedules, and close monitoring. We recommend making the process owner responsible and accountable for making changes and achieving the desired results. If you have decided to reorganize around processes (see Chapter 8), now is the time to start making the "process owner" position more powerful.

- **Change management.** Use change management methods when introducing improvements. Without them, people will resist innovation, become demoralized, and perhaps leave you in a worse situation than before. Reread Chapter 11 and substitute your recommended improvements for activity costing and management to know what to do.

- **Validation.** Use activity costing methods to validate the results of improvement. This means comparing baseline performance to the new level gained through enacting improvement recommendations. If the gains are not sufficient, find out why and take corrective action.

- **Redeploy savings.** You save nothing until you remove the resources saved by improvement from an activity. This can be hard to do when it involves people, especially in government. Even when positions are eliminated, managers will find ways of keeping the people that filled them in other newly created positions. In most government organizations, the calculus of career advancement is "the more people you manage, the more money you make." Also, no manager wants to see any part of his or her budget grow smaller, which is what happens when demand remains the same and productivity increases.

  That is why you have to plan how you will redeploy people whose positions are no longer needed. We discuss the people aspect of this in more detail in Chapter 11.

- **Publicize results.** Use all communications channels to let customers, suppliers, managers, and stakeholders know about your successes. This builds momentum for the run across home plate and back around the diamond for more scores.

Institutionalizing The New Approach

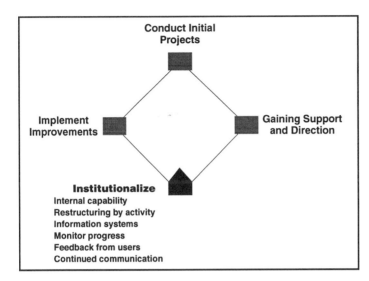

Figure 12-6
Institutionalizing
Activity-Based
Management

You've reached home plate: having been through an initial round of success, you continue to use ABC and Activity-Based Management to gain even more. To do this, you have to institutionalize these innovations.

Internal capability

ABC has a rich and varied tool box. During your first few projects using it, you probably used only a few of its tools and techniques. Over time your people will want to use more and you need to assist them. You also need to maintain the integrity of existing applications of activity methods because people may modify them in ways that degrade the methods' accuracy and validity.

Training. In the initial projects, your people practiced learning-by-doing through building activity and cost models and using activity information for process improvement. It is not a good idea, however, to have these pioneers take full charge of teaching new employees the activity approach through informal, on-the-job training. This encourages passing along mistakes and bad habits that the pioneers may have developed.

Instead, give new people a short but standard course on activity methods that is conducted by your training department or by other specialists. The best time to do this is just before managers and employees need to work on improvement projects. For example, you can make training part of an organization-wide initiative to develop activity maps, activity and cost drivers, cost models, and especially performance measures for all processes. Give short refresher courses on activity costing and management to all users every few years to hone their skills and develop new ones.

Each year, send a few accountants and managers to outside conferences and seminars on cost management, which is where most presentations on activity approaches are made today. This, plus staying up to date through articles and books, helps your organization discover ways to improve the way you use activity methods.

Restructuring by process

If you have decided to follow the principles of Activity-Based Management as outlined in Chapter 8, you will want to begin restructuring operations by process. This means appointing process managers for your major cross-functional processes, and giving them the support and resources to control and improve these processes.

In addition, you may want to reconfigure some processes by shifting activities from others into them, eliminating non-value added processes, and restructuring your operations in general. Two keys to success in this are to:

- Have a strategic plan with goals and objectives that will help guide decision-making about restructuring

- Keep track of these changes through your financial and
  management information system.

Financial and management information systems

As discussed in Chapter 7, you will eventually want to integrate ABC into your financial and management information
systems. Your new system should be able to collect data on
and produce a variety of reports about activity performance
and activity costs. You will want to introduce activity budgeting, discussed in Chapter 8, as the chief means of planning and controlling operations expenditures.

Such information system investments are major costs and
they should be carefully planned and executed. We recommend using pilot projects in single business units, field sites,
or large cross-functional processes to help develop these
systems.

Monitor performance

The best thing you can do to maintain your gains—and
make new ones—is to monitor the performance of improved
activities and all core business processes over time. Unless
you do this, performance *will* start to decay. Unneeded rules
or procedures will be added to a once streamlined activity
or training will grow lax because of other pressures, resulting in poor, uneven work execution. Good performance
measures regularly collected and reviewed will make these
problems visible.

Equally important, the world will not stand still after you
improve an activity. Outside your organization, another
organization is getting better at what you do. Some agencies
can go on for years, unaware of this external progress (or
simply ignoring it), until the inevitable happens. In the private sector, this is major loss of market share, and often
bankruptcy, as competitors forge ahead. For government
organizations, the moment of truth often comes from criticism by an oversight agency or blue-ribbon panel report.

When the report says that your organization has fallen far behind private companies in delivering the same type of service, headlines and editorials will scream, "Privatize!"

To avoid this, benchmark an improved activity's performance against the best practices of outside organizations. Use activity costing and mapping to help make the comparison, and adopt and adapt the best practices.

Feedback from users

Routinely ask activity information users about two things: how they are using the information, and how to improve its use.

The first question ensures that people are applying activity information appropriately and it may turn up some new applications. The second question targets ABC and Activity-Based Management for change so that they will improve along with the rest of your organization. The same is true for all other improvement methods and tools you use along with the activity approach.

Continued communication

As you continue to publicize the new uses and successes of ABC and Activity-Based Management you will keep them "top-of-mind" among all your people. In doing this, you reinforce behaviors that ensure continuous improvement.

And continuous improvement means winning the game.

Summary

To succeed at Activity-Based Management, you have to plan past its first applications and results. You want these initial efforts to succeed, but it is more important to lay the foundation for continuous improvement through the activity approach to management.

Of all the factors that figure into the success of Activity-Based Management, executive support is the most important. When executives "walk the walk" of Activity-Based Management, so will everyone else.

New Principles from Chapter 12

Getting Results from Activity-Based Management

Old Rule or Practice	New Principle or Practice

Old Rule or Practice	New Principle or Practice

References

1. Al Gore, remarks delivered at Harvard Commencement Day, Harvard University, Cambridge, MA, 9 June 1994.

2. Federal Accounting Standards Advisory Board "Managerial Cost Accounting Standards for the Federal Government: Statement of Recommended Accounting Standards," Exposure Draft, 7 October 1994.

3. Stephen Goldsmith, "Moving municipal services into the marketplace," No. 14 in a series of papers by Carnegie Privatization Project, Carnegie Council, New York, NY, (20 November, 1992).

4. The National Performance Review, Franchising: Essential Information. Washington, DC. (no date).

5. Joel Garreau, *The Nine Nations of North America*, (Boston: Houghton Mifflin) 1981, 105.

6. Dale R. Geiger, "An experiment in federal cost accounting and performance measurement," *The Government Accountants Journal*, Winter 1993/94:39-52.

7. Gregory D.L. Morris, "An old plant pioneers new maintenance methods," *Chemical Week*, 9 June 1993:33.

8. H. Thomas Johnson, "It's time to stop overselling activity-based concepts," *Management Accounting*, September 1992:26-35.

9. Robin Cooper and Robert S. Kaplan, *The Design of Cost Management Systems: Text, Cases, and Readings* (Englewood Cliffs, NJ: Prentice Hall), 1991.

10. Jay N. Nisberg, *The Random House Handbook of Business Terms* (New York: Random House, 1988).

11. Eliyahu M. Goldratt and Jeff Cox, *The Goal: A Process of Ongoing Improvement, Revised Edition* (Croton-on-Hudson, NY: North River Press, Inc.), 1986.

12. Robert S. Kaplan, "In defense of activity-based cost management," *Management Accounting*, November 1992: 58-63.

13. U.S. Government Accounting Office, *Quality Management: Survey of Federal Organizations*, GAO/GED-93-9B2, Washington, DC, October 1994.

14. Peter B.B. Turney, *Johnson & Johnson Medical, Inc.: A Case Series* (Portland, OR: Cost Technology, Inc.), 1993.

15. David K. Carr et al., *BreakPoint Business Process Redesign* (Washington, DC: Coopers & Lybrand), 1992.

16. Frank C. Carlucci, *Frank Carlucci on Management in Government* (Washington, DC: Center for Excellence in Government), 1987.

17. Jeffrey A. Schmidt, "Is it time to replace traditional budgeting?" *Journal of Accountancy*, October 1992:103-107.

18. The National Performance Review. *From Red Tape to Results: Creating a Government That Works Better and Costs Less*, Washington, DC: 1993.

19. Ibid.

20. Anne B. Fisher, "Welcome to the age of overwork," *Fortune*, 30 November 1992: 64-71.

21. Robert M. Tomasko, *Downsizing: Reshaping the Corporation for the Future* (New York: American Management Association), 1987.

22. H. Armitage and R. Nicholson, "Activity-based costing: A survey of Canadian practice," *CMA Magazine*, March 1993: 22.

23. T.P. Pare, "A new tool for managing costs (activity-based costing)," *Fortune*, 14 June 1993: 124-127.

24. Ibid.

25. R. Howell et al., *Cost Management For Tomorrow: Seeking The Competitive Edge* (Morristown, NJ: Financial Executives Research Foundation), 1992.

26. Ibid.

27. S. Barr. "Is there a consultant in the house?" *CFO*, September 1993: 79-84.

28. J.M. Brausch, "Selling ABC," *Management Accounting*, February 1992: 69-77.

29. David Broder, "A mayor shows Gore's team the way," *The Washington Post*, 24 August 1993.

30. Robin Cooper, Robert S. Kaplan, et al. *Implementing Activity-Based Cost Management: Moving From Analysis to Action* (Montvale, NJ: Institute of Management Accountants), 1994.

31. Ibid.

32. Geiger, An experiment in federal cost.

33. J.D. Duck "Managing change: The art of balancing," *Harvard Business Review*, November-December 1993: 109-118.

Appendix A:
Suggested Reading

Activity Costing and Management

Relevance Lost: The Rise and Fall of Management Accounting,
H. Thomas Johnson and Robert S. Kaplan, Boston: Harvard Business
School Press, 1991. 269 pages. ISBN 0-87584-254-2.

This is the "foundation" book of activity-based costing, although
ABC is not mentioned in it. Drs. Johnson and Kaplan explore "the
evolution of management accounting in American business from the
early textile mills to present-day computer-automated manufacturers..." It is a detailed exploration, one that most nonaccountants
may find unexciting, but the last four chapters are required reading
for anyone in charge of developing an ABC system. Harvard profes-
sor Kaplan is an adviser to the Federal Accounting Standards
Advisory Board, helping to develop new managerial accounting
standards that, at press time, recommend ABC.

Activity Accounting: An Activity-Based Costing Approach, James A.
Brimson, New York: John Wiley & Sons, 1991. 214 pages. ISBN 0-
471-53985-6.

Written while he was a Partner in Coopers & Lybrand's London,
England office, Brimson's first book on ABC focuses on manufacturing. It is a good first read for government organizations and contractors whose work includes industrial activities.

Activity-Based Management for Service Industries, Government Entities, and Non-Profit Organizations, James A. Brimson and John Antos, New York: John Wiley & Sons, 1994. 364 pages. ISBN 0-471-01351-X.

Despite the title this book has very few examples of government operations and is mainly geared toward for-profit companies. Still, to date this is the most extensive discussion of ABC and Activity-Based Management in service organizations. Government readers will find it an excellent reference book.

Common Cents: The ABC Performance Breakthrough, Peter B.B. Turney, Portland, OR: Cost Technology, 1993. 322 pages. ISBN 0-9629576-7.

An easy-to-read primer on ABC, Turney's is a good first book on both ABC principles and how to introduce ABC to an organization. Besides clearly explaining the technical aspects of ABC, the book outlines the change management aspects of making the transition from traditional cost accounting. This is a must-read. Cost Technology, Turney's company, also publishes several case studies that are worth reading.

Activity Dictionary, Tom Pryor, Inc., 4025 Woodland Park Blvd., Suite 390, Arlington, TX 76013, telephone 1-800-955-2233. 400 pages, 1992.

This is a generic activity dictionary with definitions of the most common activities in manufacturing. These include support functions such as accounting, advertising, computers, engineering, general administration, human resources, legal, marketing, materials management, quality, sales, and research and development. Each activity listing includes potential cost drivers, inputs and outputs, and other information (see Figure 4-2 for an example page). Although the $100 price for this book seems high, having it is better than starting from scratch.

The following books can be ordered from the Institute of Management Accounting, Special Orders Department, 10 Paragon Drive, Montvale, NJ 07645-1760, telephone 800-638-4427, fax 201-573-9507. IMA offers its members a 20 percent discount on these books.

Implementing Activity-Based Cost Management: Moving From Analysis to Action, Robin Cooper, Robert S. Kaplan, et al., Montvale, NJ: Institute of Management Accountants, 1994. 336 pages. ISBN 0-86641-206-9.

More case studies, this time focusing on the process of introducing ABC in eight manufacturing companies. There are many lessons to be learned in this book about the perils and pitfalls of making the transition to ABC. Although the lessons are summarized in the last chapter, people in charge of introducing ABC or Activity-Based Management should read the whole book.

Activity-Based Management in Action: The Development, Unfolding and Progression of ABC Management Systems, edited by Patrick L. Romano, Montvale, NJ: Institute of Management Accountants, 1993. 160 pages. ISBN 0-86641-227-1.

Order this collection of 25 reprints of articles on ABC and Activity-Based Management, and save money and time doing literature searches.

Total Quality Management

Excellence in Government: Total Quality Management in the 1990s, second edition, David K. Carr and Ian D. Littman, Washington, DC: Coopers & Lybrand, 1992. 353 pages. ISBN 0-944533-07-8.

With more than 35,000 copies sold, this is the most popular book on TQM in government, and also the most comprehensive (it discussed ABC in the public sector in its first edition in 1989). It contains more than 150 examples of TQM in the public sector, including defense and civilian agencies and national, state, and local government. Any process improvement methodology not discussed in detail in *Activity-Based Management in Government* will be found in *Excellence in Government,* or in the following book.

Process Improvement: A Guide for Teams, Clifton Cooksey, Debra Eshelman, Richard Beans, Washington, DC: Coopers & Lybrand, 1993. 246 pages. ISBN 0-944533-06-X.

How do teams of managers and workers make improvements to the problems and opportunities identified by ABC? This is a how-to manual covering how to scope an improvement project, develop baseline data, analyze problems and opportunities, generate and test improvements, and introduce them to operations. Its "tool box" includes detailed instructions on more than 40 tools and techniques for improvement such as statistical process control tools, brain-storming, and affinity diagrams. Each manual includes a computer disk and user guide of software programs for dozens of statistical tools discussed in the text.

Benchmarking

Benchmarking: A Tool For Continuous Improvement, C.J. McNair and Kathleen H.J. Leibfried, Essex Junction, VT: Omneo, 1992. 344 pages. ISBN 0-939246-53-8.

A comprehensive, practical guide to developing quantitative and qualitative benchmarks for process improvement. Rich with examples, it is an ideal starting point for examining the performance of internal as well as external comparison processes.

Change Management

Managing Change: Opening New Organizational Horizons, David K. Carr, Kelvin Hard, and William J. Trahant. Washington, DC: Coopers & Lybrand, 1994. 284 pages. ISBN 0-944533-12-4 (hardback) ISBN 0-944533-16-7 (paperback).

An in-depth exploration of the art and science of managing change in organization, this book provides dozens of examples from government and industry. Chapter 11 of this book was based on the methods and techniques presented in *Managing Change*. The authors are partners in Coopers & Lybrand's Washington, DC and London, England offices.

Performance Measurement

Customer Service Measurement, Monograph Series #1, David Wilkerson and Clifton Cooksey, Washington, DC: Coopers & Lybrand, 1994. 72 pages. ISBN 0-944533-08-6.

A handy guide to determining customer expectations and levels of satisfaction, then linking the results to performance measures at the process level. Geared toward government organizations, it contains examples from the public sector.

Survey Assessment, Monograph Series #2, David Wilkerson and Jefferson Kellogg, Washington, DC: Coopers & Lybrand, 1994. 63 pages. ISBN 0-944533-09-4.

This monograph discusses the steps involved in using survey instruments to collect information on customer expectations and satisfaction, and personnel morale, climate, and culture.

Measure Up! Yardsticks for Continuous Improvement, Richard L. Lynch and Kelvin F. Cross, Cambridge, MA: Blackwell, 1991. 213 pages. ISBN 1-55786-099-8.

Both Tom Peters and Dr. Robert Kaplan endorse this easy-to-read, practical overview of modern performance measurement. It shows the limitations of traditional measures and how to develop a new system that captures all aspects of operations performance.

Reengineering

BreakPoint Business Process Redesign: How America's Top Companies Blast Past the Competition, David K. Carr, Kevin S. Dougherty, Henry J. Johansson, Robert E. King, and David E. Moran, Washington, DC: Coopers & Lybrand, 1992. 206 pages. ISBN 0-944533-04-3.

An overview of business process redesign or reengineering (BPR), discussed in Chapter 3 of *Activity-Based Management in Government*, this book discusses using activity-based costing in BPR, and the relationship of BPR to information technology, quality management, and change management. It presents a methodology for developing, introducing, and sustaining major changes.

Business Process Reengineering: BreakPoint Strategies for Market Dominance, Henry J. Johansson, Patrick McHugh, A. John Pendlebury, and William A. Wheeler III. West Sussex, UK: John Wiley, 1993. 241 pages. ISBN 0-471-93883-1.

The authors are partners in Coopers & Lybrand offices in the U.S. and the U.K. More technical than *BreakPoint Business Process Redesign*, this book follows the same methodology. It provides more details on global organizations and manufacturing. It's a "must-read" for any government industrial or technical operation that is considering reengineering.

All books published by Coopers & Lybrand in Washington, DC, may be ordered from:

> Bookmasters, Inc.
> Distribution Center
> 1444 State Rt. 42
> RD 11
> Mansfield, Ohio 44903
> Telephone: 1-800-247-6553
> Fax: 419-281-6883

Appendix B:
Questions to Ask When Planning for Activity-Based Costing and Activity-Based Management

Shared Values and Vision

What new beliefs about your organization will be necessary to make the change?

What perceptions or traditions will be broken or built?

How will people learn about and understand the goals and expectations of using ABC or practicing Activity-Based Management?

How will individuals and groups be rewarded and recognized for successfully making the change? What if they do not or cannot make the change?

What incentives will be used to promote the desired behaviors of the new way of doing business?

Strategy

What new elements of strategy are required to support the change (i.e., strategic commitment to continuous improvement, change in product pricing strategy)?

How will the change fit with other activities or changes?

How will ABC or Activity-Based Management affect current business plans?

How will ABC or Activity-Based Management integrate with your organization's operating principles?

Structure

How will the structure of your organization or any individual departments change to align with the change?

How will reporting or power structures change?

How will people be expected to use ABC information or follow Activity-Based Management principles to accomplish their work? Individually? In teams?

What new behavior or skills will be required for people to successfully use ABC or practice Activity-Based Management?

How will jobs or job groups be different from the way they are now?

What span of control would best support the change?

Systems

As a result of ABC or Activity-Based Management, what new information will be available to make effective business decisions?

What expectations will exist for people to be able to create or act on ABC information? What tools will they have to do this?

What level of performance in using ABC or following Activity-Based Management principles is expected?

How will this performance be measured?

How will new systems, such as costing or process performance measurement, be integrated with existing systems?

What feedback mechanisms will be affected by the change?

What modifications or additions should be devised to support the change?

Work Processes

What will the new ABC process, or the processes associated with Activity-Based Management, look like? Where do these processes begin and end? Where do they reside?

Who will "own" each process and be responsible for its performance?

What resources will ABC or Activity-Based Management require?

People and Skills

What knowledge, skills, or abilities will people need to make and sustain the change?

How will they obtain new knowledge, skills, or abilities?

Will new employees, or new types of employees, be needed to operate the ABC system or work under the principles of Activity-Based Management?

What level or degree of flexibility will be required of employees and managers?

How will learning and using new skills be integrated into existing programs and training?

Leadership and Culture

What observable behaviors will leaders be expected to display?

What will be the relationship between supervisors and employees? Coach? Inspector? Team leader? (This question is especially important in Activity-Based Management.)

What new management skills or abilities will managers and supervisors need?

What new tasks will managers and supervisors be expected to perform?

What cultural norms will be affected by the change?

Glossary

Activity: A unit of work that has identifiable starting and ending points, that consumes *resources* (inputs) and produces *outputs*. In ABC, an activity is synonymous with a simple *process*, as the latter term is used in quality management and reengineering.

Activity analysis: The study of activity performance and the causes for variation in performance, done in order to improve operations.

Activity-Based Costing (ABC): A set of managerial accounting methods used to identify and describe *cost object* and the *activities* they consume, and the amount of *resources* the activities consume.

Activity-based management: Business management in which *process owners* have the responsibility and authority to control and improve operations, and that uses ABC methods.

Activity budgeting: The use of ABC methods to prepare operations budgets to show the amount of resources that identified activities are expected to consume, based on forecasted demand for their outputs.

Activity center: A list of all activities that support or benefit a specific *cost object*, and the costs associated with those activities.

Activity costing: see *activity-based costing*.

Activity dictionary: A list and description of all activities in an organization, which often includes information on each activity's location, *performance measure*, and *attribute*.

Activity driver: A factor that influences the frequency or intensity with which a *cost object* consumes activity outputs.

Activity level: Describes which part of an operation an activity supports, and also indicates its nature. Activity levels include:

- *Unit* activities are done for every unit of output produced by a process. Putting letters into envelopes is a unit activity done on every letter mailed.

- *Batch* activities are done on a group of outputs. Carrying boxes of letters to a mailbox is a batch activity.

- *Customer* activities are done to support individual or groups of customers. This would include communicating with a customer, answering complaints, or arranging certain services.

- *Organization* activities are done to support an entire organization. Preparing strategic plans is an organization activity.

Activity management: see *Activity-Based Management.*

Activity model: A report that describes the related activities of a *process*, organization, or *activity center.*

Allocating: In cost accounting, the practice of assigning costs according to a formula, as opposed to directly *tracing* them to those activities, products, or services that consume these costs (cf. *tracing*).

As-is process model: A verbal or graphic description of a *process* as it is now being done, sometimes accompanied by information on the *process' cost*, cycle-time, or other measures of performance. A *to-be process model* describes how the process will look and perform once it is changed.

Attribute: A characteristic of an *activity*, i.e., it is value added or non-value added; belongs to one of the four categories of *cost-of-quality*; etc.

Batch activity: see *activity level.*

Benchmarking: A process improvement method used to understand an existing *activity process*, then to identify an external point of reference by which that activity can be measured and judged.

Bill of activities: A list of the activities consumed by a *cost object*, along with their costs and other information.

Business process redesign: Completely redesigning or reengineering a process to achieve a new, much higher standard of performance.

Capacity: The volume of products or services an organization can produce given existing *resources*.

Core business process: A *process*, usually cross-functional, that produces an organization's main products or services.

Cost driver: A factor that causes activity performance to vary in a way that results in the activity's consuming fewer or greater amounts of *resources*.

Cost model: A report on the cost of a set of related activities.

Cost object: The reason an activity exists, i.e., one or more products, services, projects, or *customers*.

Cost-of-quality: An analysis that groups certain types of activities into four categories (prevention, appraisal, internal failure, external failure) and sums the costs of each category.

Cross-functional process: A process that occurs in more than one organizational *function*, department, or other major work unit.

Culture: The basic assumptions and beliefs that are shared by members of an organization, that operate unconsciously, and define in a "taken for granted" fashion an organization's view of itself and its environment.

Customer: (1) External users of an organization's products or services, (2) internal users of an activity or process outputs.

Customer level activity: see *activity level.*

Enterprise process: A very large macro-process, the various parts of which are done in several different organizations that collectively form an enterprise.

Full-time equivalent (FTE): A measure of labor hours, e.g., two people who work half time at a task make one FTE.

Function: A work unit in an organization that provides a certain type of service or other, e.g., accounting, distribution, planning, purchasing, production.

Indirect costs: see *overhead.*

Inputs: Information and materials that flow into an activity or process that are transformed within the activity into outputs.

Just-in-time: (1) An approach to managing production that is designed to manufacture just the amount of products immediately required by customers; (2) in training, having trainees learn new practices just before they need to use them.

Organizational activity: see *activity level.*

Outputs: Products and services (including work-in-progress) that flow out of an activity or process, and information about them.

Overhead: Also known as indirect costs, these are costs that cannot be assigned exclusively to any particular product, project, process, or activity. In traditional cost accounting, overhead includes most support services. ABC takes a much narrower view of overhead and strives to include only *organizational activities* in it.

Performance measure: A financial or non-financial indicator that is causally related to and varies with the performance of an activity, product, or service, and that can be used in decisions to control or improve that activity.

Process: A set of logically related activities done to achieve a defined

business outcome, such as to produce a product or service.
See *activity*.

Process owners: Managers who are in charge of the control and improvement of specific processes. (cf. *Activity-Based Management*).

Process simulation: Running trials of *"as-is"* and *"to-be"* models to test "what-if" assumptions about process improvement and *reengineering*.

Quality management: An approach to process control and improvement that focuses on meeting customer expectations, reducing process variation, and continuous improvement.

Reengineering: see *business process redesign*.

Relational data base: In ABC, a computerized data base of *activities* that allows the activities and their assigned costs to be easily aggregated into different *activity centers*, work units, or *attributes*.

Resources: Money, labor, material, supplies and other economic elements consumed by *activities* to produce outputs.

Support activity: see *activity level*.

Time-based management: An approach to process improvement that focuses on reducing cycle times.

To-be process model: See *as-is process model*.

Tracing: The practice of assigning costs to *activities* based on their actual consumption of these costs (cf. *allocating*).

Traditional cost accounting: Product costing and managerial accounting systems that rely primarily on *allocation* to assign indirect or overhead costs to activities, products, and services.

Unit activity: see *activity level*.

Value analysis: An analysis that categorizes *activities* according to whether they add value to the output of an activity or process. Value added activities transform work-in-process in ways that customers perceive as beneficial. Non-value added activities either do not transform work-in-process or transform it in ways that customers do not perceive as beneficial.

About the Authors

Joseph Kehoe

Joe is C&L's industry leader and managing partner for the Government Services Practice. In his 20 years with Coopers & Lybrand, Joe has directed dozens of engagements involving cost management systems and helped to develop the firm's activity-based costing practice. As partner-in-charge of C&L's work with the Naval Industrial Improvement Program, he helped the Navy save more than $1 billion through management improvements. Joe pioneered the use of Activity-Based Management in major organizational restructuring and is an adviser on ABC to the Federal Accounting Standards Advisory Board. He holds a BS in accounting from the University of Virginia and an MBA in finance from Syracuse University.

William Dodson

As a C&L partner, Bill works with the U.S. Navy shipyards and other public and private organizations to introduce ABC and Activity-Based Management. Before joining C&L, he worked for 20 years with two Fortune 500 corporations, holding the positions of manager of budgeting and financial reporting, controller, distribution manager, plant manager, vice president, and Chief Financial Officer. Bill holds a BS in business administration from Virginia Polytechnic Institute and State University and an MBA from the University of Virginia.

Robert Reeve

Bob, a managing associate, has more than 20 years of public and private sector experience in operations and management improvement. He worked with Navy shipyards, EG&G Mound Nuclear, and the U.S. Postal Service in applying Activity-Based Management to improving operations. Other clients include the Department of Energy, Department of Defense, Army, Navy, Air Force, Department of Housing and Urban Development, and the Social Security Administration. He earned a BS in industrial administration from Iowa State University and an MBA from the University of Virginia.

Gustav Plato

Gus, a managing associate, has more than 10 years of management consulting experience, plus five years working with retail companies. His Activity-Based Management clients include the U.S. Postal Service and the Navy, and he has worked with the Defense Commissary Agency, George Washington University, Air Force, Agency for International Development, Commonwealth of Virginia, and the government of Latvia on management improvement projects. Gus holds a BS degree in economics from George Mason University.

About Coopers & Lybrand L.L.P.

Founded in 1898, Coopers & Lybrand L.L.P. is one of the Big Six accounting and management consulting firms. It is one of the largest in size, with extensive resources in all major cities throughout the world.

C&L's Government Services Practice in Washington, DC, includes 400 professionals engaged in performance improvement projects in local, state, and national government in the U.S. and overseas. In addition, the practice works with Fortune 500 corporations, major universities, and nonprofit organizations. In the past five years, this practice has worked with more than 100 federal organizations to introduce quality management, activity-based costing, and improved information, financial, and operations management systems.

For more information on Coopers & Lybrand's government and government contractor services, contact:

Coopers & Lybrand L.L.P.
1530 Wilson Boulevard
Arlington, VA 22209
Telephone: 703-908-1500
Fax: 703-908-1695

Index

Notes